SOA Lecture Series (Applied Physics)
COM, Momentum And Collisions

(Black And White Edition)

Er Vinay Shanker Shukla
Author

ABOUT THE PAPERBACK (BLACK AND WHITE EDITION)
BY THE AUTHOR

Nowadays one can get hundreds of live online videos delivering lectures on physics. This makes it very difficult to revise the video content during periodical tests and school exams/engineering or medical entrance exams. Keeping this point in his mind he has created this **SOA Lecture Series** on **Applied Physics**. This book will be very useful for the preparation of **(10+2)/IIT-JEE (main & advanced)/NEET(UG)/SAT Subject Test/KVPY/NTSE/Olympiads** to be held all over the world. This lecture series is already delivered by him in the classroom of **SIGMA PHYSICS CENTRE** Allahabad (UP) India. You will find it summarized like class notes which makes this book different from textbook content. The complete **Black And White Edition** is written in a chapterwise single book. **Black And White Edition** is much cheaper than the multicoloured edition. **Black And White Edition** has two parts:

(i) Analytical supplement (ii) Tryout Supplement

ANALYTICAL SUPPLEMENT: This is the summarized version of the original lecture delivered in his classroom. You can find the complete analysis, derivation, graphical approach, graphical analysis, numerical illustrations of toughness level-1, 2, & 3 along with the labelled diagrams of the whole prescribed syllabus.

TRYOUT SUPPLEMENT: This section consists of two level question bank archives for practice purpose:

(i)Galaxy: JEE (main)/SAT Subject Test archive

(ii)Universal: IIT-JEE (advanced)/KVPY/NTSE/Olympiads archive

with great love,
Er Vinay Shanker Shukla
B Tech (Civil Engg)
IIT-BHU Varanasi, INDIA

ABOUT THE AUTHOR

Er Vinay Shanker Shukla (Instructor of Applied Physics) is the author of the book **SOA Lecture Series (Applied Physics)** in the format of **PAPERBACK (Black And White Edition)**. He is B Tech (Civil Engg) with DGPA: 8.43/10.00 from IIT-BHU Varanasi, INDIA.

He has thirty plus years of teaching experience in his own academy **SIGMA PHYSICS CENTRE** Allahabad (UP) India. He was the founder and the head instructor at this institute. To know more about his

Er Vinay Shanker Shukla
B Tech (Civil Engg)
IIT-BHU Varanasi,
INDIA

academic journey, you may look up **SOA Lecture Series (Applied Physics)** over at Google, Facebook, and LinkedIn.

To order or subscribe **SOA Lecture Series (Applied Physics)** you can visit the websites **amazon.in, flipkart.in, amazon.com, flipkart.com** and **notionpress.com**.

To watch video explanation of his books free of cost you can browse his YouTube channel **Vinay Shanker Shukla** and get benefitted.

Best wishes to the aspirants of **IIT-JEE (main & advanced)/NEET (UG)/SAT Subject Test/KVPY/NTSE/Olympiads** and **(10+2)** students all over the world. **GOOD LUCK!**

THIS IS MANDATORY TO LEARN
PHYSICAL MATHEMATICS
AND WORK, ENERGY, POWER
BEFORE READING THIS BOOK.

PREFACE TO THE BOOK SOA LECTURE SERIES

I am truly impressed with this series: **SOA Lecture Series (Applied Physics)**. These are spectacular tools for anyone seriously preparing for the exams like **IIT-JEE, NEET(UG)** or even the **Olympiads**.

What I particularly appreciate is the enormous number of problems included: varied, well-chosen, and with an approach that truly helps develop physical intuition and agility in problem solving.

It's clear that they are designed with a wealth of teaching experience of **Mr Vinay Shanker Shukla** behind them. These are not books to be read passively, but to be worked on and practiced intensively. If you're looking for a solid collection to level up your applied physics, this series is, without a doubt, an excellent choice.

Highly recommended!

Written by:
Dr. de Enrique Arribas Garde
Professor at UCLM in Albacete, Spain.
Author of the book **"Solved Electromagnetic Problems"**
Dated: 27/03/2025

INDEX

ANALYTICAL SUPPLEMENT

This chapter is divided into four parts:

1.0. Centre Of Mass And Centre Of Gravity

2.0. Momentum

3.0. Collisions Or Impacts

4.0. Numerical Examples

1.0. CENTRE OF MASS AND CENTRE OF GRAVITY

1.1. DEFINITION

Centre of mass of a rigid body or many particle system or many body system is defined as a point (either inside the solid portion or outside the solid portion) at which the whole mass of the system can be assumed to be concentrated and the line of action of the resultant force passes through it during the pure translational motion of the body.

Centre of gravity of a rigid body or many particle system or many body system is defined as a point (either inside the solid portion or outside the solid portion) at which the whole weight (gravity force) of the system can be assumed to be acting.

1.2. VARIOUS PROPERTIES OF CENTRE OF MASS

1.2.1. Many Particle System:

(i) Position Vector Of COM:

See the below figure for the reference. Consider N particle system where $m_1, m_2, m_3, \ldots m_N$ are their masses and $\vec{r}_1, \vec{r}_2, \vec{r}_3 .. \vec{r}_N$ are their position vectors then the position vector $\vec{r}_{CM}$ of the COM of the system is defined as:

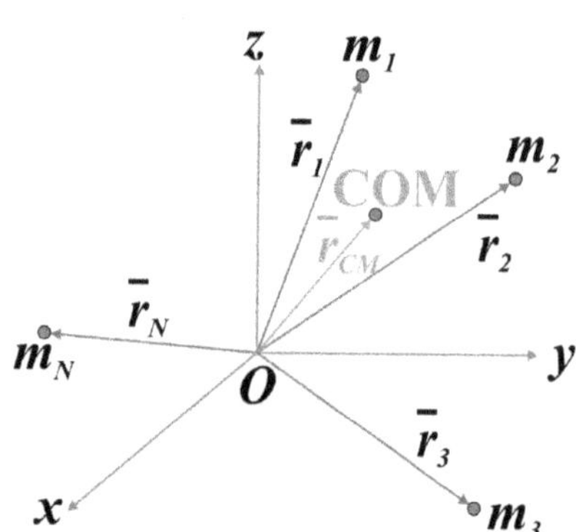

$$\vec{r}_{CM} = \frac{\Sigma\,(m_i \vec{r}_i)}{\Sigma (m_i)} = \frac{m_1\vec{r}_1 + m_2\vec{r}_2 + m_3\vec{r}_3 + \ldots\ldots m_N\vec{r}_N}{m_1 + m_2 + m_3 + \ldots\ldots + m_N}$$

(ii) Velocity Vector Of COM: See the below figure for the reference. Consider N particle system where m_1, m_2, m_3,.... m_N are their masses and $\vec{v}_1, \vec{v}_2, \vec{v}_3,........\vec{v}_N$ are their velocity vectors then the velocity vector $\vec{v}_{CM}$ of the COM of the system is defined as:

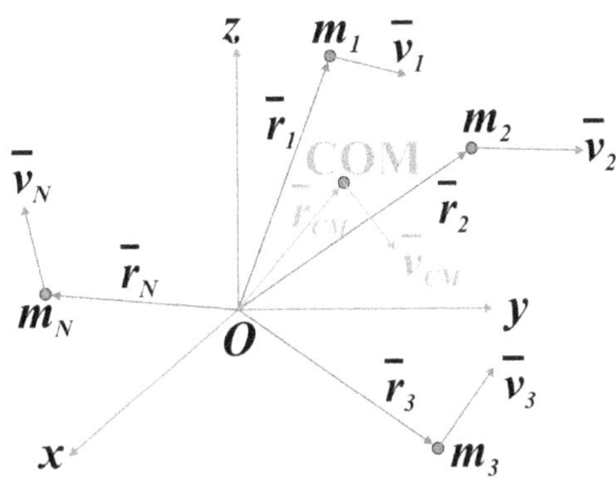

$$\vec{v}_{CM} = \frac{d\vec{r}_{CM}}{dt} = \dot{\vec{r}}_{CM} = \frac{d}{dt}\left(\frac{m_1\vec{r}_1 + m_2\vec{r}_2 + m_3\vec{r}_3 + ...m_N\vec{r}_N}{m_1 + m_2 + m_3 + ...+ m_N}\right)$$

$$= \frac{m_1\dfrac{d\vec{r}_1}{dt} + m_2\dfrac{d\vec{r}_2}{dt} + m_3\dfrac{d\vec{r}_3}{dt} + ...+ m_N\dfrac{d\vec{r}_N}{dt}}{m_1 + m_2 + m_3 + ...+ m_N}$$

$$\vec{v}_{CM} = \frac{m_1\vec{v}_1 + m_2\vec{v}_2 + m_3\vec{v}_3 + ...+ m_N\vec{v}_N}{m_1 + m_2 + m_3 + ...+ m_N} = \frac{\Sigma(m_i\vec{v}_i)}{\Sigma(m_i)}$$

(iii) Acceleration Vector Of COM: See the next figure for the reference. Consider N particle system where m_1, m_2, m_3,.... m_N are their masses and $\vec{a}_1, \vec{a}_2, \vec{a}_3,........\vec{a}_N$ are their acceleration vectors then the acceleration vector $\vec{a}_{CM}$ of the COM of the system is defined as:

$$\vec{a}_{CM} = \frac{d\vec{v}_{CM}}{dt} = \frac{d^2\vec{r}_{CM}}{dt^2} = \dot{\vec{v}}_{CM} = \ddot{\vec{r}}_{CM} = \frac{\Sigma(m_i\vec{a}_i)}{\Sigma(m_i)}$$

$$\vec{a}_{CM} = \frac{d\vec{v}_{CM}}{dt} = \frac{d}{dt}\left(\frac{m_1\vec{v}_1 + m_2\vec{v}_2 + m_3\vec{v}_3 + \ldots\ldots + m_N\vec{v}_N}{m_1 + m_2 + m_3 + \ldots\ldots + m_N}\right)$$

$$= \frac{m_1\dfrac{d\vec{v}_1}{dt} + m_2\dfrac{d\vec{v}_2}{dt} + m_3\dfrac{d\vec{v}_3}{dt} + \ldots\ldots + m_N\dfrac{d\vec{v}_N}{dt}}{m_1 + m_2 + m_3 + \ldots\ldots + m_N}$$

$$\vec{a}_{CM} = \frac{m_1\vec{a}_1 + m_2\vec{a}_2 + m_3\vec{a}_3 + \ldots\ldots + m_N\vec{a}_N}{m_1 + m_2 + m_3 + \ldots\ldots + m_N} = \frac{\Sigma(m_i\vec{a}_i)}{\Sigma(m_i)}$$

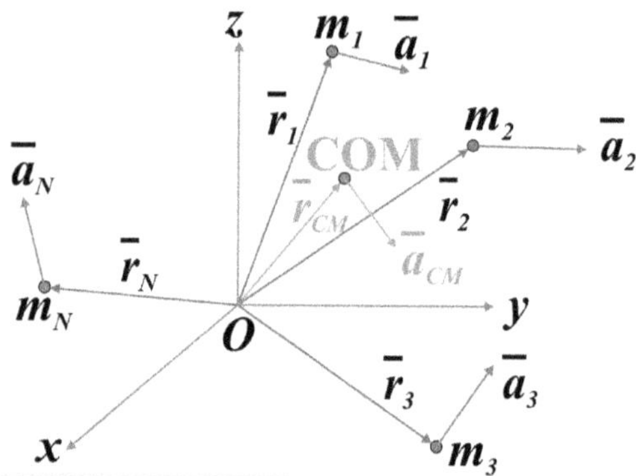

(iv)Jerk Vector Of COM: See the below figure for the reference. Consider N particle system where m_1, m_2, m_3, …. m_N are their masses and $\vec{\beta}_1, \vec{\beta}_2, \vec{\beta}_3, \ldots\ldots \vec{\beta}_N$ are their jerk vectors then the jerk vector $\vec{\beta}_{CM}$ of the COM of the system is defined as:

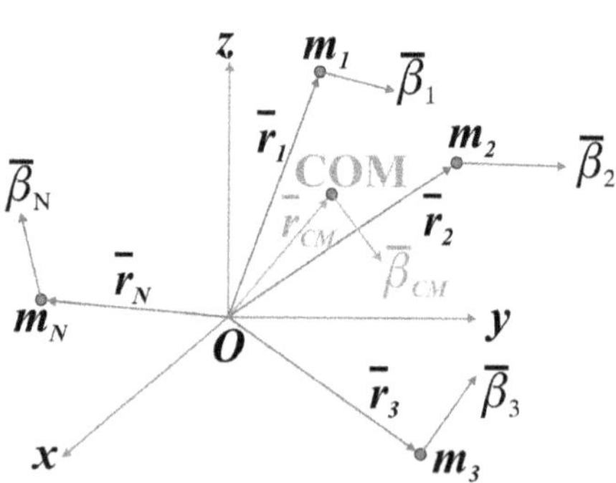

$$\vec{\beta}_{CM} = \frac{d\vec{a}_{CM}}{dt} = \frac{d^2\vec{v}_{CM}}{dt^2} = \frac{d^3\vec{r}_{CM}}{dt^3} = \dot{\vec{a}}_{CM} = \ddot{\vec{v}}_{CM} = \dddot{\vec{r}}_{CM} = \frac{\Sigma\left(m_i\vec{\beta}_i\right)}{\Sigma(m_i)}$$

$$= \frac{d\vec{a}_{CM}}{dt} = \frac{d}{dt}\left(\frac{m_1\vec{a}_1 + m_2\vec{a}_2 + m_3\vec{a}_3 + \ldots\ldots\ldots + m_N\vec{a}_N}{m_1 + m_2 + m_3 + \ldots\ldots\ldots + m_N}\right)$$

$$= \frac{m_1\dfrac{d\vec{a}_1}{dt} + m_2\dfrac{d\vec{a}_2}{dt} + m_3\dfrac{d\vec{a}_3}{dt} + \ldots\ldots\ldots + m_N\dfrac{d\vec{a}_N}{dt}}{m_1 + m_2 + m_3 + \ldots\ldots\ldots + m_N}$$

$$\vec{\beta}_{CM} = \frac{m_1\vec{\beta}_1 + m_2\vec{\beta}_2 + m_3\vec{\beta}_3 + \ldots\ldots\ldots + m_N\vec{\beta}_N}{m_1 + m_2 + m_3 + \ldots\ldots\ldots + m_N} = \frac{\Sigma(m_i\vec{\beta}_i)}{\Sigma(m_i)}$$

(v)Cartesian Co-Ordinates Of COM: Consider N particle system where m_1, m_2, m_3,…. m_N are their masses and (x_1,y_1,z_1), (x_2,y_2,z_2), (x_3,y_3,z_3)…….. (x_N,y_N,z_N) are their position co-ordinates then the position co-ordinates (x_{CM},y_{CM},z_{CM}) of the COM of the system is defined as:

$$x_{CM} = \frac{\Sigma\left(m_i x_i\right)}{\Sigma\left(m_i\right)} = \frac{m_1 x_1 + m_2 x_2 + m_3 x_3 + \ldots\ldots + m_N x_N}{m_1 + m_2 + m_3 + \ldots\ldots + m_N}$$

$$y_{CM} = \frac{\Sigma\left(m_i y_i\right)}{\Sigma\left(m_i\right)} = \frac{m_1 y_1 + m_2 y_2 + m_3 y_3 + \ldots\ldots + m_N y_N}{m_1 + m_2 + m_3 + \ldots\ldots + m_N}$$

$$z_{CM} = \frac{\Sigma\left(m_i z_i\right)}{\Sigma\left(m_i\right)} = \frac{m_1 z_1 + m_2 z_2 + m_3 z_3 + \ldots\ldots + m_N z_N}{m_1 + m_2 + m_3 + \ldots\ldots + m_N}$$

(vi)Linear Momentum Of COM: See the next figure for the reference. Consider N particle system where m_1, m_2, m_3,….. m_N are their masses; $\vec{r}_1,\vec{r}_2,\vec{r}_3,\ldots\ldots\vec{r}_N$ are their position vectors; $\vec{p}_1,\vec{p}_2,\vec{p}_3,\ldots\ldots\vec{p}_N$ are their linear momentum vectors then the linear momentum vector $\vec{p}_{CM}$ of the COM of the system is defined as:

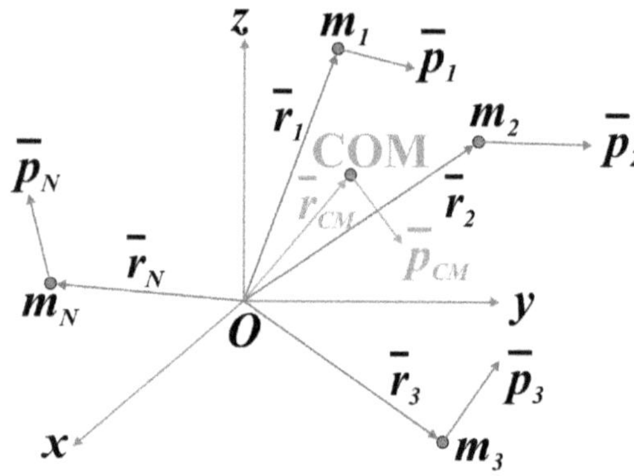

$$\vec{p}_{CM} = \left(\sum m_i\right)\vec{v}_{CM} \text{ but } \vec{v}_{CM} = \frac{\sum m_i\vec{v}_i}{\sum m_i}, \text{ hence } \vec{p}_{CM} = \left(\sum m_i\right)\frac{\sum m_i\vec{v}_i}{\sum m_i}$$

$$\rightarrow \vec{p}_{CM} = \sum m_i\vec{v}_i = \sum \vec{p}_i = \vec{p}_1 + \vec{p}_2 + \vec{p}_3 + \ldots\ldots + \vec{p}_N = \vec{p}_{system}$$

(vii)Gravitational Potential Energy Of COM: See the below figure for the reference. Consider N particle system where m_1, m_2, m_3,….. m_N are their masses. Suppose xy plane is a vertical plane and y-axis is the vertical axis. Suppose x-axis is the horizontal reference datum for the measurement of the gravitational potential energy of the various particles shown and also suppose that the gravitational field is uniform, that is $\vec{g}$ vector is constant everywhere and directed vertically downwards. Suppose $y_1, y_2, y_3\ldots\ldots y_N$ are the respective heights of the particles above the reference datum shown. Then the gravitational potential energy U_{CG} of the COM of the system will be:

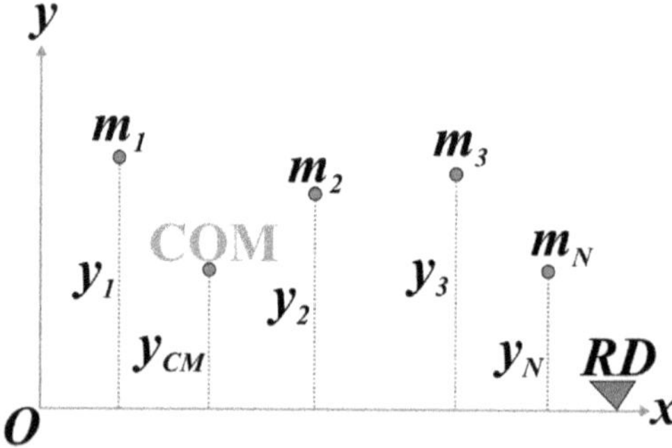

$$U_{CG} = \left(\sum m_i\right) g y_{CG} = \left(\sum m_i\right) g \frac{\sum m_i y_i}{\sum m_i} = g \sum m_i y_i = \sum m_i g y_i$$

$$\rightarrow U_{CG} = \sum m_i g y_i = \sum U_i = U_1 + U_2 + U_3 + \dots + U_N = U_{system}$$

(viii)Kinetic Energy Of COM: See the below figure for the reference. Consider N particle system where m_1, m_2, m_3,…. m_N are their point masses and $\vec{v}_1, \vec{v}_2, \vec{v}_3, \dots \vec{v}_N$ are their velocity vectors and $\vec{v}_{CM}$ is the velocity vector of the COM of the system, then the kinetic energy of the COM of the system is defined as:

$$K_{CM} = \frac{1}{2}\left(\sum m_i\right) v_{CM}^2 \text{ but } v_{CM} = \left|\vec{v}_{CM}\right| = \left|\frac{\sum m_i \vec{v}_i}{\sum m_i}\right| = \frac{\left|\sum m_i \vec{v}_i\right|}{\sum m_i}$$

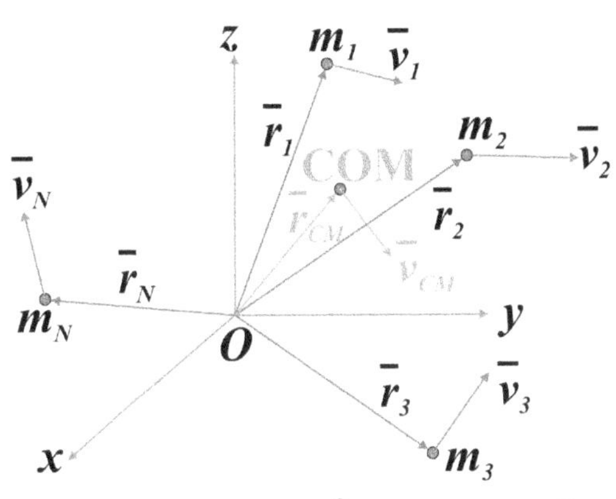

$$\rightarrow K_{CM} = \frac{1}{2}\left(\sum m_i\right)\left(\frac{\left|\sum m_i \vec{v}_i\right|}{\sum m_i}\right)^2 = \frac{1}{2}\frac{\left|\sum m_i \vec{v}_i\right|^2}{\sum m_i} - (i)$$

$$K_{system} = K_1 + K_2 + K_3 + \dots + K_N = \sum K_i = \sum \frac{1}{2} m_i v_i^2 - (ii)$$

From eq (i) & (ii), it is evident that: $K_{CM} \neq K_{system}$

1.2.2. Rigid Body System: See the below figure for the reference. Suppose for the given rigid body, (x_{CM}, y_{CM}, z_{CM}) are the co-ordinates of the COM. A big rigid body can be assumed to be composed of infinitesimally small elements compacted together. Such a system is called **continuum**. For a continuum system, the mass of a particular particle is written as dm; and its co-ordinates are written as (x, y, z). The symbol Σ is replaced by $\int$ for the continuum system. Thus, the co-ordinates of COM of the rigid body system can be expressed as:

$$x_{CM} = \frac{\Sigma(m_i x_i)}{\Sigma(m_i)} = \frac{\int(dm)x}{\int(dm)}, y_{CM} = \frac{\Sigma(m_i y_i)}{\Sigma(m_i)} = \frac{\int(dm)y}{\int(dm)}, z_{CM} = \frac{\Sigma(m_i z_i)}{\Sigma(m_i)} = \frac{\int(dm)z}{\int(dm)}$$

1.2.3. Centre Of Mass Of A Cut Body: For the residual body:

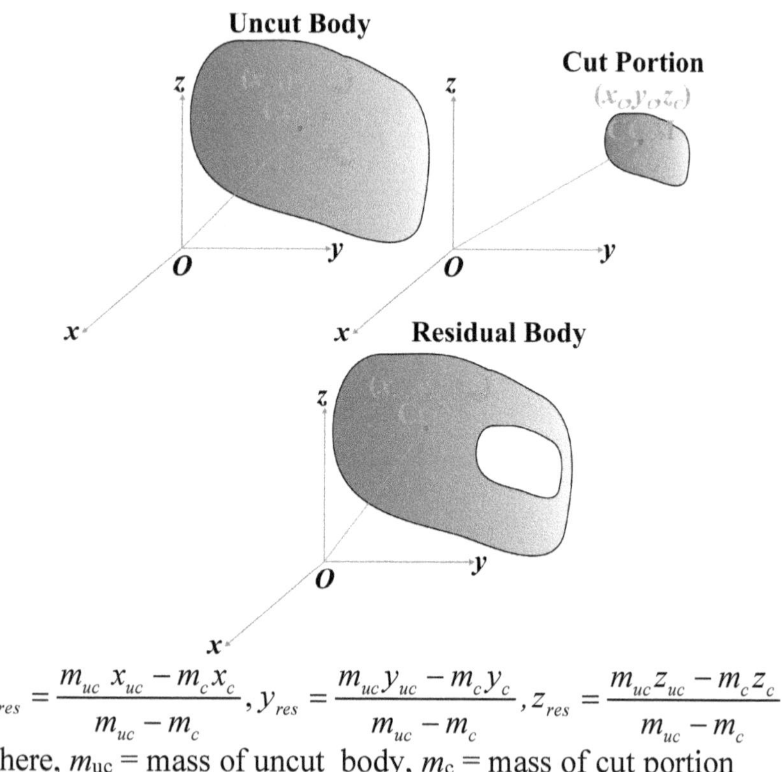

$$x_{res} = \frac{m_{uc}\, x_{uc} - m_c\, x_c}{m_{uc} - m_c}, y_{res} = \frac{m_{uc}\, y_{uc} - m_c\, y_c}{m_{uc} - m_c}, z_{res} = \frac{m_{uc}\, z_{uc} - m_c\, z_c}{m_{uc} - m_c}$$

where, m_{uc} = mass of uncut body, m_c = mass of cut portion

(x_{uc}, y_{uc}, z_{uc}) = co-ordinates of COM of uncut body
(x_u, y_c, z_c) = co-ordinates of COM of cut portion of the main body
$(x_{res}, y_{res}, z_{res})$ = co-ordinates of COM of the residual body
See the below and next figures for the reference.

1.2.4. Centre Of Mass Of Some Important Solids:

(i) Solid Cone (Uniform Mass-Density):

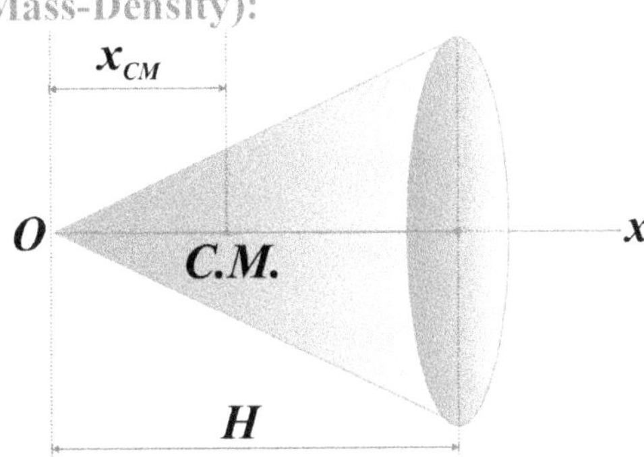

$$x_{CM} = \frac{3}{4}H$$

(ii) Uniform Ring Segment:

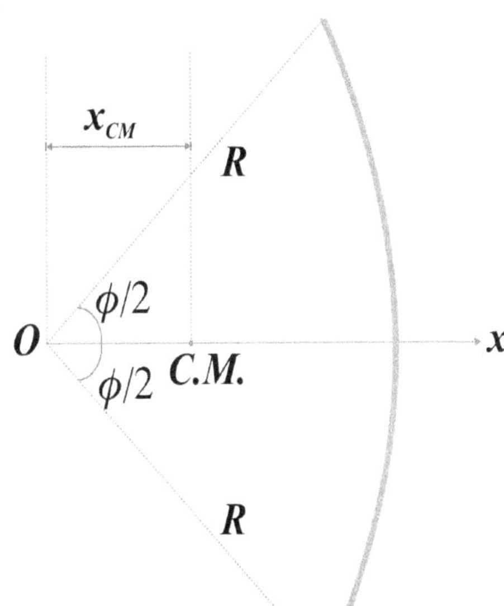

$$x_{CM} = R\left[\frac{\sin\dfrac{\phi}{2}}{\dfrac{\phi}{2}}\right]$$

For half ring, $\phi = \pi$, $x_{CM} = \dfrac{2R}{\pi}$

For quarter ring, $\phi = \pi/2$

$$x_{CM} = R\left[\frac{\sin\dfrac{\pi/2}{2}}{\dfrac{\pi/2}{2}}\right] = \frac{4R}{\pi}\left[\frac{1}{\sqrt{2}}\right]$$

$$\rightarrow x_{CM} = \frac{2\sqrt{2}R}{\pi}$$

(iii)Radial Segment Of A Uniform Disc:

$$x_{CM} = \frac{4}{3}R\left[\frac{\sin\frac{\phi}{2}}{\phi}\right];$$

For half disc, $\phi=\pi$

$$x_{CM} = \frac{4R}{3\pi}$$

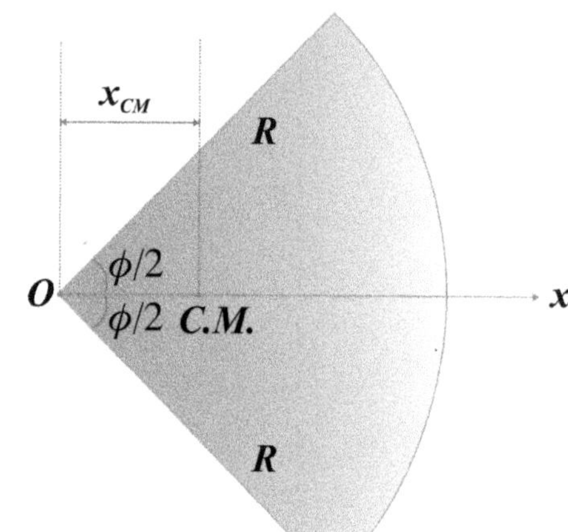

(iv)Frustum Of A Thin Spherical Shell:

$$x_{CM} = \frac{R}{2}\left[\frac{\left(\sin\frac{\phi}{2}\right)^2}{\left(1-\cos\frac{\phi}{2}\right)}\right]; \quad \left(\begin{array}{l}\text{For hemispherical} \\ \text{shell:} \\ \phi=\pi \rightarrow x_{CM} = \frac{R}{2}\end{array}\right)$$

$$x_{CM} = \frac{R}{2}\left[\frac{\left(\sin\frac{\pi}{2}\right)^2}{\left(1-\cos\frac{\pi}{2}\right)}\right] = \frac{R}{2}\left[\frac{(1)^2}{(1-0)}\right] = \frac{R}{2}$$

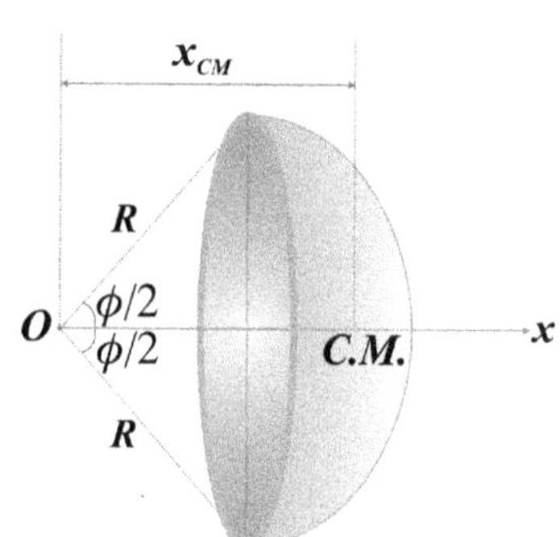

(v)Uniform Triangular Lamina:

$$x_{CM} = \frac{H}{3}$$

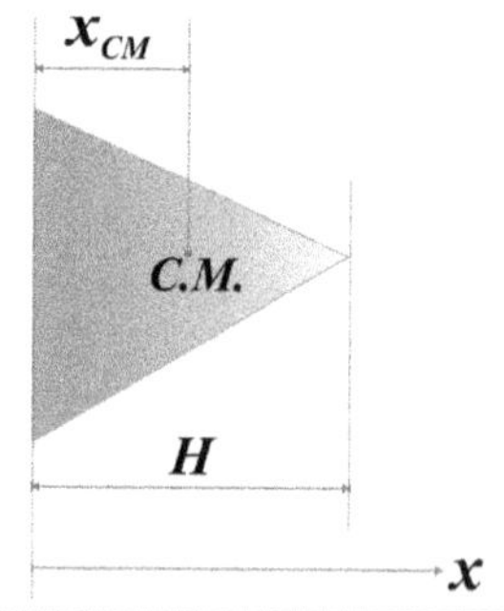

(vi)Solid Homogeneous Hemisphere:

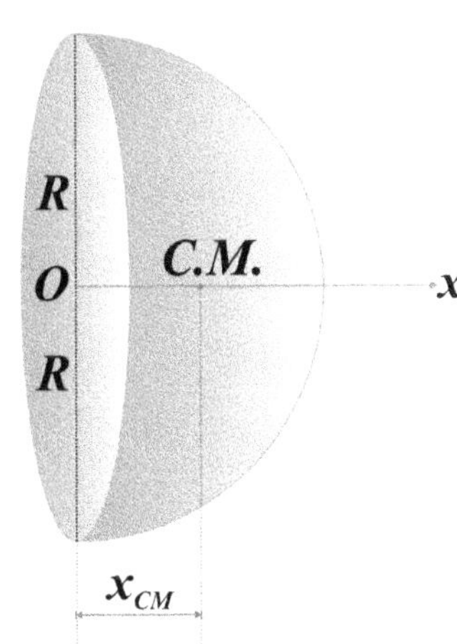

$$x_{CM} = \frac{3R}{8}$$

(vii)Uniform Conical Shell Without Base:

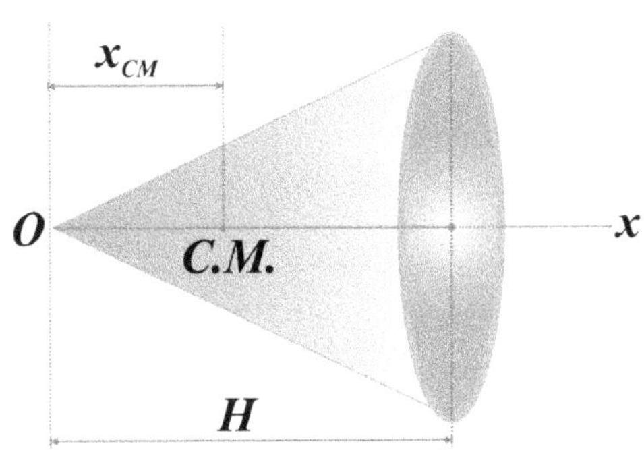

$$x_{CM} = \frac{2H}{3}$$

1.3.POSITION PARAMETERS OF CENTRE OF GRAVITY

1.3.1.Many Particle System: Consider N particle system where w_1, w_2, w_3,…..w_N are their weights and $\vec{r_1}, \vec{r_2}, \vec{r_3},.......\vec{r_N}$ are their position vectors then the position vector $\vec{r}_{CG}$ of the COG of the system is defined as:

(i)Position Vector Of COG:

$$\vec{r}_{CG} = \frac{\Sigma\,(w_i \vec{r_i})}{\Sigma(w_i)} = \frac{w_1 \vec{r_1} + w_2 \vec{r_2} + w_3 \vec{r_3} + ……….+ w_N \vec{r_N}}{w_1 + w_2 + w_3 + ……….+ w_N}$$

(ii)Cartesian Co-Ordinates of COG:

$$x_{CG} = \frac{\Sigma(w_i x_i)}{\Sigma(w_i)}, y_{CG} = \frac{\Sigma(w_i y_i)}{\Sigma(w_i)}, z_{CG} = \frac{\Sigma(w_i z_i)}{\Sigma(w_i)}$$

1.3.2.Rigid Body System:

$$x_{CG} = \frac{\int(dw)x}{\int dw}, y_{CG} = \frac{\int(dw)y}{\int dw}, z_{CG} = \frac{\int(dw)z}{\int dw}$$

NOTE: Under uniform gravitational field, COM and COG both are co-incident but under non-uniform gravitational field, COM & COG are different.

2.0. MOMENTUM

2.1.DEFINITION

Momentum vector or linear momentum vector $\vec{p}$ of a particle is defined as the product of its mass m and velocity vector $\vec{v}$, that is: $\vec{p} = m\vec{v}$.

Momentum vector or linear momentum vector $\vec{p}_{system}$ of many particle system is defined as the vector sum of individual momentum of each particle, that is:

$$\vec{P}_{system} = \sum_{i=1}^{i=N} m_i \vec{v}_i = m_1\vec{v}_1 + m_2\vec{v}_2 + m_3\vec{v}_3 + \dots\dots\dots + m_N\vec{v}_N$$

$$\rightarrow \vec{P}_{system} = \vec{p}_1 + \vec{p}_2 + \vec{p}_3 + \dots\dots\dots + \vec{p}_N = \sum_{i=1}^{i=N} \vec{p}_i$$

2.2.PRINCIPLE OF CONSERVATION OF LINEAR MOMENTUM OF CENTRE OF MASS

According to the Newton's second law : $\sum \vec{F}_{ext} = \dfrac{d\vec{p}_{CM}}{dt}$

If $\sum \vec{F}_{ext} = \vec{0} \Rightarrow \dfrac{d\vec{p}_{CM}}{dt} = \vec{0} \Rightarrow \vec{p}_{CM} = $ constant or conserved.

In the absence of external forces, if initial $\vec{p}_{CM} = \vec{0}$, then final

$$\vec{p}_{CM} = \vec{0} \Rightarrow \Sigma\left(m_i\vec{v}_i\right) = \vec{0} \Rightarrow \Sigma\left(m_i\frac{d\vec{r}_i}{dt}\right) = \vec{0} \Rightarrow \Sigma\left(m_i d\vec{r}_i\right) = \vec{0}$$

In component form, we can write that:

If $\left(F_{ext}\right)_x = 0$ and initial $\left(p_{CM}\right)_x = 0$, then $\Sigma\left(m_i dx_i\right) = 0$

$$\Rightarrow \Sigma\left(m_i \Delta x_i\right) = 0 \Rightarrow m_1\Delta x_1 + m_2\Delta x_2 + m_3\Delta x_3 + ... + m_N\Delta x_N = 0$$

Similarly, we can get results for y and z components as:

If $\left(F_{ext}\right)_y = 0$ and initial $\left(p_{CM}\right)_y = 0$, then $\Sigma\left(m_i dy_i\right) = 0$

$$\Rightarrow \Sigma\left(m_i \Delta y_i\right) = 0 \Rightarrow m_1\Delta y_1 + m_2\Delta y_2 + m_3\Delta y_3 + ... + m_N\Delta y_N = 0$$

If $\left(F_{ext}\right)_z = 0$ and initial $\left(p_{CM}\right)_z = 0$, then $\Sigma\left(m_i dz_i\right) = 0$

$$\Rightarrow \Sigma\left(m_i \Delta z_i\right) = 0 \Rightarrow m_1\Delta z_1 + m_2\Delta z_2 + m_3\Delta z_3 + ... + m_N\Delta z_N = 0$$

These are the most important conditions to be used in the numerical problems.

3.0. COLLISIONS

3.1. CLASSIFICATION BASED UPON THE KINETIC ENERGY CONSERVATION

In this chapter this is general assumption that all the external forces acting on the system of colliding bodies is much less than the internal impulsive forces during the collision, hence the linear momentum of the system will remain conserved during the collision. On the basis of kinetic energy conservation, collisions are divided into three parts:

(i) **Elastic Impact:** In this type of impact, the total kinetic energy of the colliding bodies just before impact and just after impact becomes equal. The coefficient of restitution (e) becomes equal to 1. Total mass of the colliding bodies and their temperature remain conserved.

(ii) **Semi Elastic Impact:** In this type of impact, the total kinetic energy of the colliding bodies just before impact becomes greater than the total kinetic energy just after impact.

The loss of kinetic energy gets converted into elastic potential energy and heat energy. The coefficient of restitution (e) becomes less than 1. Total mass of the colliding bodies remains conserved but their temperature does not remain conserved.

(iii) **Inelastic Impact:** In this type of impact, the total kinetic energy of the colliding bodies just before impact becomes much greater than the total kinetic energy just after impact. The loss of kinetic energy gets converted into elastic potential energy and heat energy. The coefficient of restitution (e) becomes equal to zero. Total mass of the colliding bodies remains conserved but their temperature does not remain conserved.

3.2. COLLISIONS OR IMPACT OF ROUND BODIES

In this case if two frictionless rigid spherical/cylindrical bodies collide with each other, then the line of impact passes through the line joining their centres. We have two classifications:

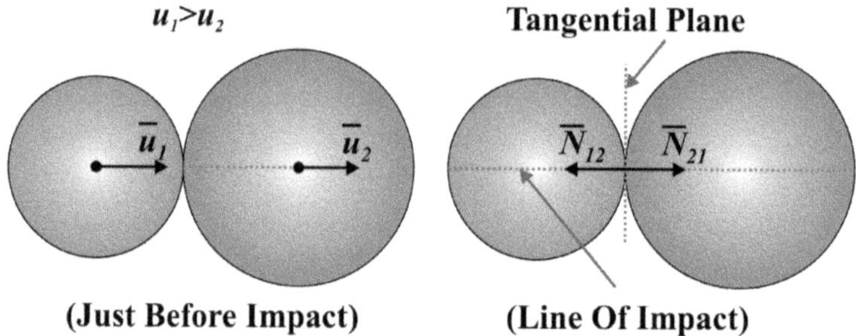

(Just Before Impact)   **(Line Of Impact)**

(i) **Direct Central Impact:** All velocity vectors of the colliding bodies must be collinear and oriented along the line of impact. See the previous figure for the reference.

(ii) **Oblique Central Impact:** At least one of the velocity vectors of the colliding bodies must be non collinear and not oriented along the line of impact. See the next figure for reference.

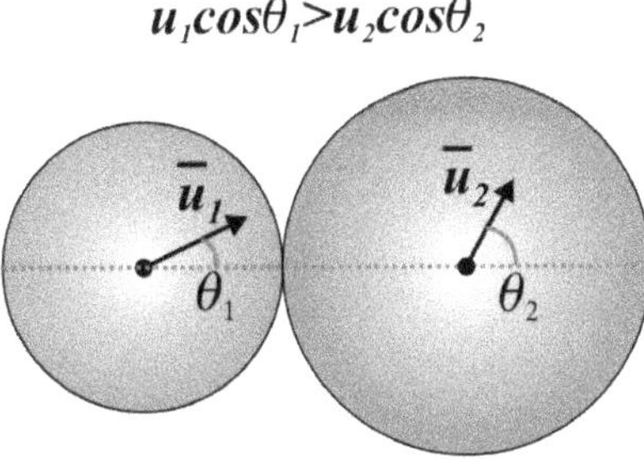

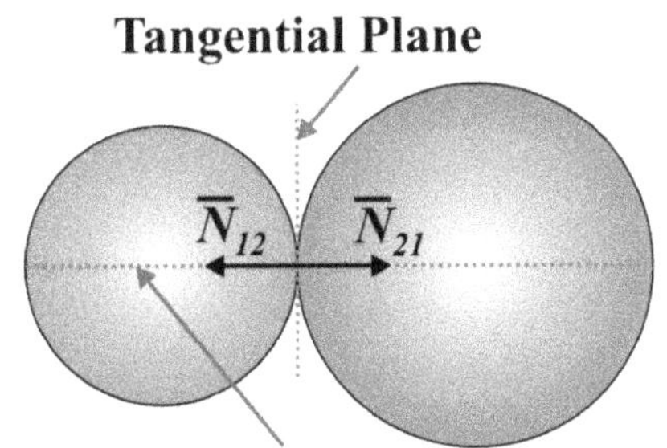

(Just Before Impact)   **(Line Of Impact)**

3.2.1. Direct Central Impact: Direct central impact has three types:

(i) Perfectly Elastic Impact: Linear momentum, KE, mass and temperature of the colliding system remain conserved just before impact and just after impact. Coefficient of restitution (e) is **unity** which is defined as:

$$e = \frac{|\text{ velocity of recession}|}{|\text{velocity of approach}|} = \frac{v_2 - v_1}{u_1 - u_2} = 1 \rightarrow (v_2 - v_1) = (u_1 - u_2) - (i)$$

[The above equation is also called Newton's Equation.]

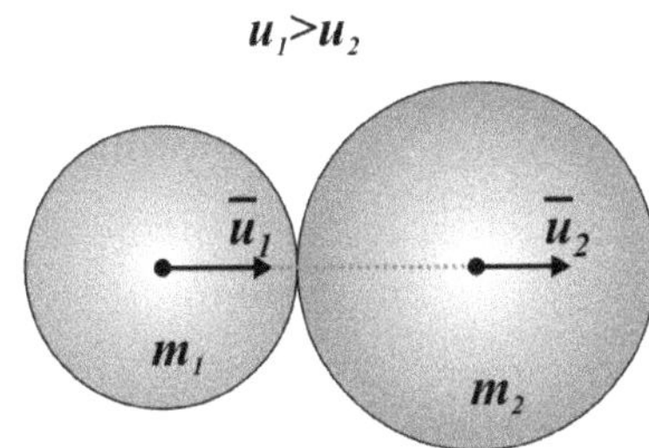

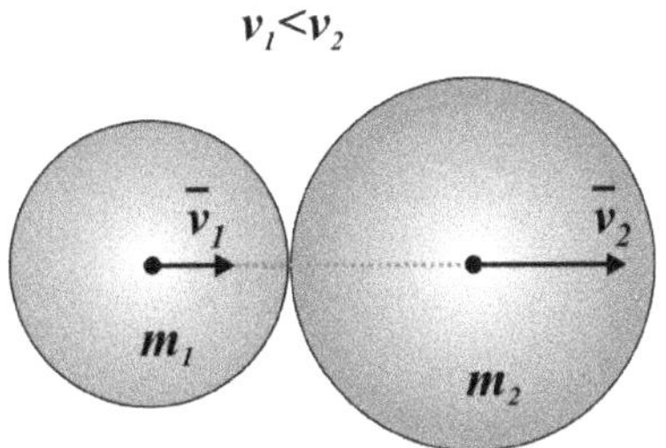

(Just Before Impact)   **(Just After Impact)**

Applying the principle of linear momentum conservation:

$$m_1 u_1 + m_2 u_2 = m_1 v_1 + m_2 v_2 - (ii)$$

(ii) Semi Elastic Impact: Only linear momentum and mass of the colliding system remain conserved. (0< e <1)

Applying the principle of linear momentum conservation:

$$m_1 u_1 + m_2 u_2 = m_1 v_1 + m_2 v_2 \quad -(i)$$

Newton's Equation:

$$(v_2 - v_1) = e(u_1 - u_2) \quad \text{or} \quad K_{final} / K_{initial} = n < 1 - (ii)$$

(iii) Inelastic Impact: Only linear momentum and mass of the colliding system remain conserved. (e = 0)

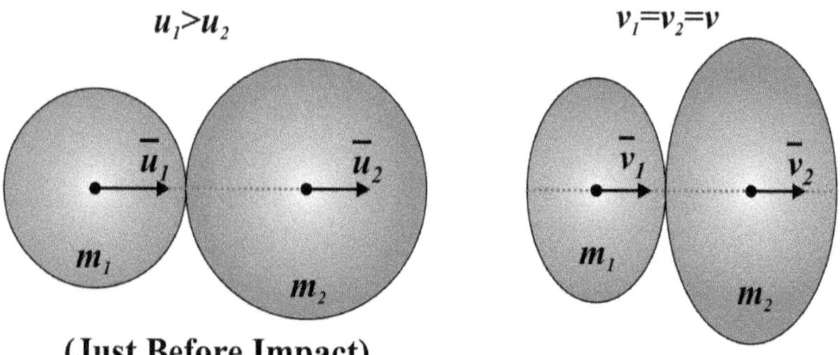

(Just Before Impact)   **(Just After Impact)**

Applying the principle of linear momentum conservation:

$$m_1 u_1 + m_2 u_2 = m_1 v_1 + m_2 v_2 \quad - (i)$$

Newton's Equation:

$$(v_2 - v_1) = (0)(u_1 - u_2) = 0 \rightarrow v_2 = v_1 = v \text{ (say)}$$

$$\text{or} \quad K_{final} / K_{initial} = n << 1 - (ii)$$

3.2.2. Oblique Central Impact: Oblique central impact has three types:

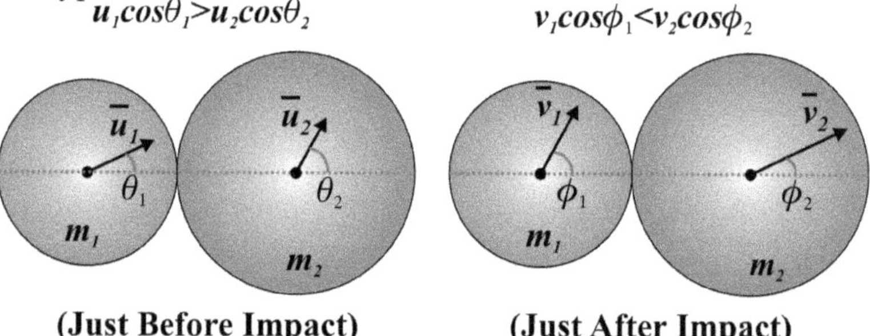

(Just Before Impact)   **(Just After Impact)**

(i) Perfectly Elastic Impact: Linear momentum, KE, mass and temperature of the colliding system remain conserved just before impact and just after impact. Coefficient of restitution(e) is unity. See the next figure for the reference.

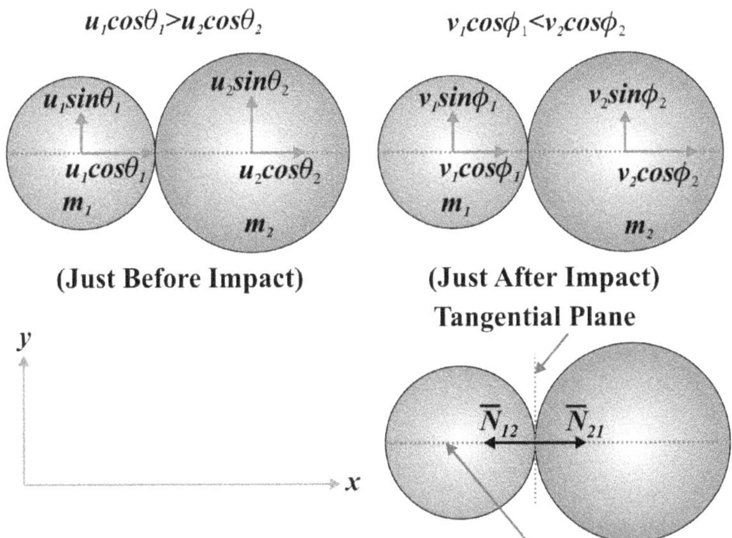

(Just Before Impact)   (Just After Impact)

Tangential Plane

(Line Of Impact)

Applying the principle of linear momentum conservation:
According to the Newton's equation:
Speed of recession: $(v_2\cos\phi_2 - v_1\cos\phi_1) = e(u_1\cos\theta_1 - u_2\cos\theta_2)$ -(iii)

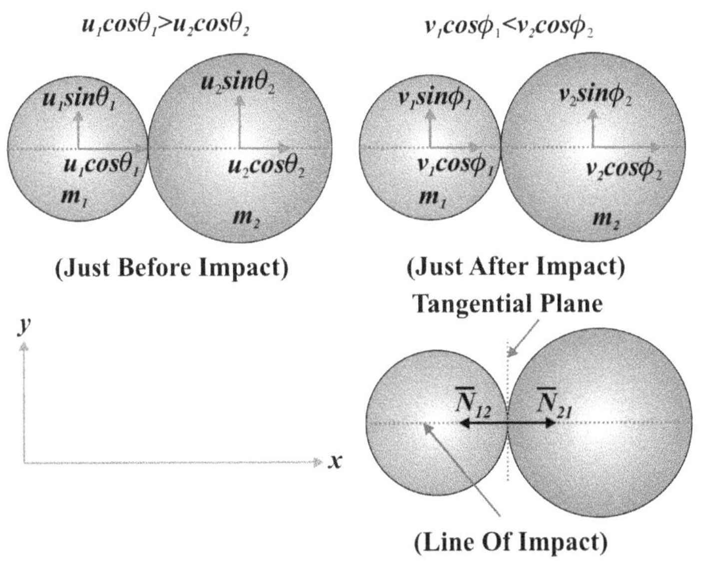

(Just Before Impact)   (Just After Impact)

Tangential Plane

(Line Of Impact)

In vector form : $\quad m_1\vec{u}_1 + m_2\vec{u}_2 = m_1\vec{v}_1 + m_2\vec{v}_2$

In the component form :

Along x – axis :

$$m_1u_1\cos\theta_1 + m_2u_2\cos\theta_2 = m_1v_1\cos\phi_1 + m_2v_2\cos\phi_2 - (i)$$

Along y – axis :

$$u_1\sin\theta_1 = v_1\sin\phi_1 - (ii) \qquad u_2\sin\theta_2 = v_2\sin\phi_2 - (iii)$$

$\left(\begin{array}{l}\text{Since there is no force component along } y - \text{axis, hence}\\ \text{along } y - \text{axis velocity component of each body will}\\ \text{remain conserved.}\end{array}\right)$

Newton's Equation :

$$(v_2\cos\phi_2 - v_1\cos\phi_1) = e(u_1\cos\theta_1 - u_2\cos\theta_2)$$

$$\rightarrow (v_2\cos\phi_2 - v_1\cos\phi_1) = (1)(u_1\cos\theta_1 - u_2\cos\theta_2) - (iv)$$

(ii) Semi Elastic Impact: Only linear momentum and mass of the colliding system remain conserved. $(0< e <1)$. Above first three equations will be similar but the fourth equation will be written as given below. See the previous figure for the reference. Applying the principle of linear momentum conservation:

In vector form : $\quad m_1\vec{u}_1 + m_2\vec{u}_2 = m_1\vec{v}_1 + m_2\vec{v}_2$

In the component form : Along x – axis :

$$m_1u_1\cos\theta_1 + m_2u_2\cos\theta_2 = m_1v_1\cos\phi_1 + m_2v_2\cos\phi_2 - (i)$$

Along y – axis : $u_1\sin\theta_1 = v_1\sin\phi_1 - (ii)$ $u_2\sin\theta_2 = v_2\sin\phi_2 - (iii)$

$\left(\begin{array}{l}\text{Since there is no force component along } y - \text{axis, hence}\\ \text{along } y - \text{axis, sum of velocity component of each body will}\\ \text{remain conserved.}\end{array}\right)$

Newton's Equation :

$$(v_2 \cos\phi_2 - v_1 \cos\phi_1) = e(u_1 \cos\theta_1 - u_2 \cos\theta_2) - (iv)$$

(iii) Inelastic Impact: Only linear momentum and mass of the colliding system will remain conserved. (e = 0)
    Above first three equations will be similar but the 4th, equation will be written as given above on this page. See the below figure for reference.

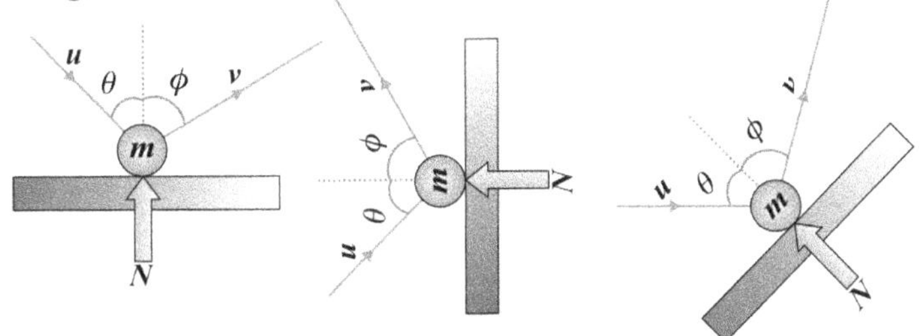

According to the Newton's equation:
|Velocity of recession|=e|Velocity of approach|
That is: $v\cos\phi = eu\cos\theta \rightarrow v\cos\phi = (1)u\cos\theta \rightarrow v\cos\phi = u\cos\theta$ –(ii)
We already know that for perfectly elastic impact e=1.
Applying the principle of linear momentum conservation:
In vector form : $\quad m_1\vec{u}_1 + m_2\vec{u}_2 = m_1\vec{v}_1 + m_2\vec{v}_2$

In the component form :

Along x – axis :

$$m_1 u_1 \cos\theta_1 + m_2 u_2 \cos\theta_2 = m_1 v_1 \cos\phi_1 + m_2 v_2 \cos\phi_2 - (i)$$

Along y – axis :

$$u_1 \sin\theta_1 = v_1 \sin\phi_1 - (ii) \qquad u_2 \sin\theta_2 = v_2 \sin\phi_2 - (iii)$$

$\left(\text{Since there is no force component along } y - \text{axis, hence} \right.$
$\quad \text{along } y - \text{axis sum of velocity component of each body}$
$\left. \quad \text{will remain conserved.} \right)$

Newton's Equation :

$$(v_2 \cos\phi_2 - v_1 \cos\phi_1) = e(u_1 \cos\theta_1 - u_2 \cos\theta_2)$$
$$\rightarrow (v_2 \cos\phi_2 - v_1 \cos\phi_1) = (0)(u_1 \cos\theta_1 - u_2 \cos\theta_2) = 0$$
$$\rightarrow v_2 \cos\phi_2 = v_1 \cos\phi_1 - (iv)$$

3.3.MISCELLANEOUS TYPES OF COLLISION
3.3.1.Collision Of A Body With Plane And Hard Surface:

Suppose a small body of mass m strikes with a plane and hard surface with speed u at a striking angle θ and rebounds with speed v at rebounding angle ϕ as shown in the next figure, also suppose that the collision is very strong and the plane surface is perfectly rigid. All external forces are negligible as compared to the normal reaction N as shown in the next figure.

(i)Perfectly Elastic Impact: Consider the small body of mass m as a system. The only dominating external force is N. The component of N parallel to the plane is zero. Hence the velocity component parallel to the plane will remain conserved. That is:
$v\sin\phi=u\sin\theta -(i)$
According to the Newton's equation:
Velocity of recession=e(Velocity of approach)
That is: $v\cos\phi=eu\cos\theta \rightarrow v\cos\phi=(1)u\cos\theta \rightarrow v\cos\phi=u\cos\theta -(ii)$
We already know that for perfectly elastic impact e=1.

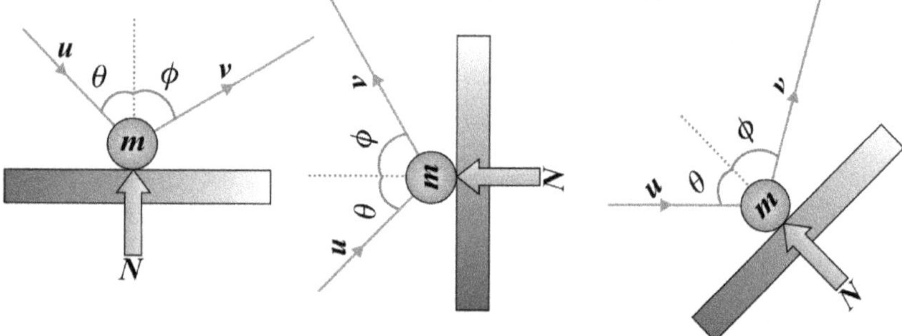

On solving these two equations, we get: $\phi=\theta$ and $v=u$
(ii)Semi Elastic Impact:

$$v\sin\phi = u\sin\theta -(i) \qquad v\cos\phi = e(u\cos\theta) -(ii)$$

[Here 0<e<1 for semi elastic impact.]

from eq(i) & (ii), we get:

$$\tan\phi = \frac{\tan\theta}{e} \rightarrow \phi = \tan^{-1}\left(\frac{\tan\theta}{e}\right) \text{ and } v = u\sqrt{\sin^2\theta + e^2\cos^2\theta}$$

(iii) Inelastic Impact:

$$v\sin\phi = u\sin\theta \quad -(i)$$

$$v\cos\phi = e\left(u\cos\theta\right) \rightarrow v\cos\phi = (0)\left(u\cos\theta\right)$$

$$\rightarrow v\cos\phi = 0 \rightarrow \cos\phi = 0 \rightarrow \phi = 90^0 \quad -(ii)$$

[Here e = 0 for inelastic impact.]

3.3.2. Collision Of A Small Body With A Massive Constrained Body: It is assumed that m<<M, (m+M)g<<N and mg<<N_1, where N_1 is the reaction force (contact force) applied by the massive trolley upon the small particle, normal to the top inclined surface. It is also assumed that all the surfaces are frictionless. The massive trolley (M) is constrained to move along the horizontal direction only and it does not rebound in the vertical direction.

Suppose just before the collision starts, the velocity vectors of M and m are $\vec{v}_1$ and $\vec{u}$ and just after the collision completes, their velocity vectors are $\vec{v}_2$ and $\vec{v}$ respectively. See the next fig (a) and fig (b) for the reference. Suppose the striking angle and the rebounding angle for the particle m are θ and ϕ respectively as shown in the next fig (a).

As shown in the next fig (d), the only significant force acting on the particle m is N_1 along y' axis, hence the velocity components of m along x' axis will be the same. That is:

$$u\sin\theta = v\sin\phi - (i)$$

Applying Newton's equation along y' axis that is the 'Line Of Impact':

|vel of recession|=e|vel of approach|, e=coeff. of restitution

$$\rightarrow (v\cos\phi - v_2\sin\alpha) = e(u\cos\theta + v_1\sin\alpha) - (ii)$$

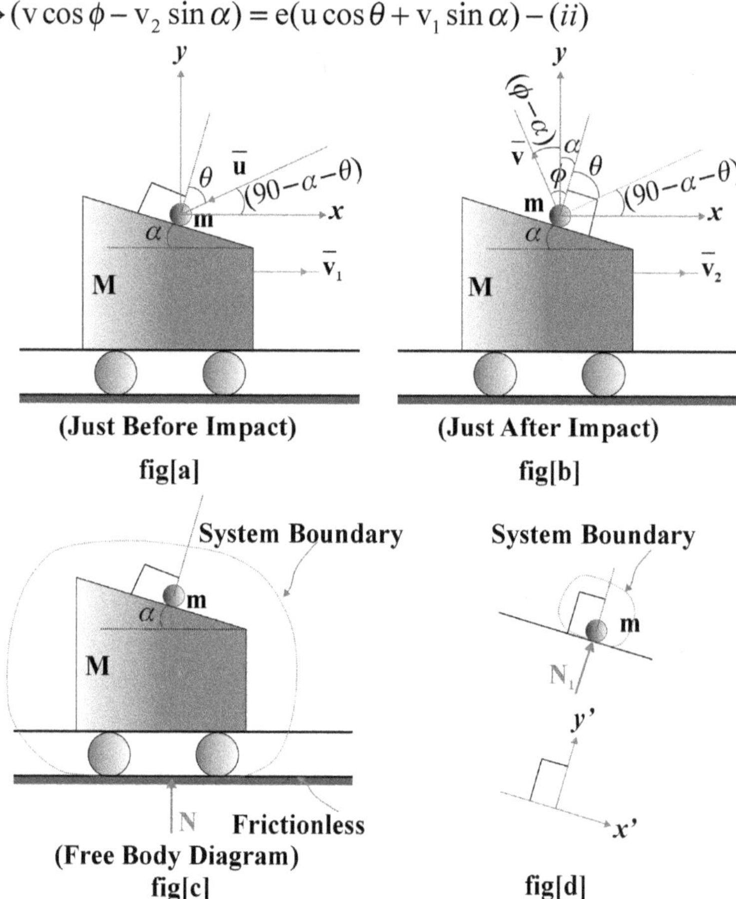

See the above fig(c) for the reference. Consider (M+m) as a system. Since the only significant external force acting is N, hence the linear momentum of (M+m) system along the *x*-axis will remain conserved, because there is no force acting along *x*-axis. That is:

$$-mu\cos(90-\alpha-\theta) + Mv_1 = Mv_2 - mv\sin(\phi-\alpha) - (iii)$$

Using these three equations, we can solve any three unknowns.

3.3.3. Eccentric Impact:

If the line of impact shown in the below fig[c] does not pass through the line joining the centre of mass of the colliding bodies then such type of impact is called eccentric impact.

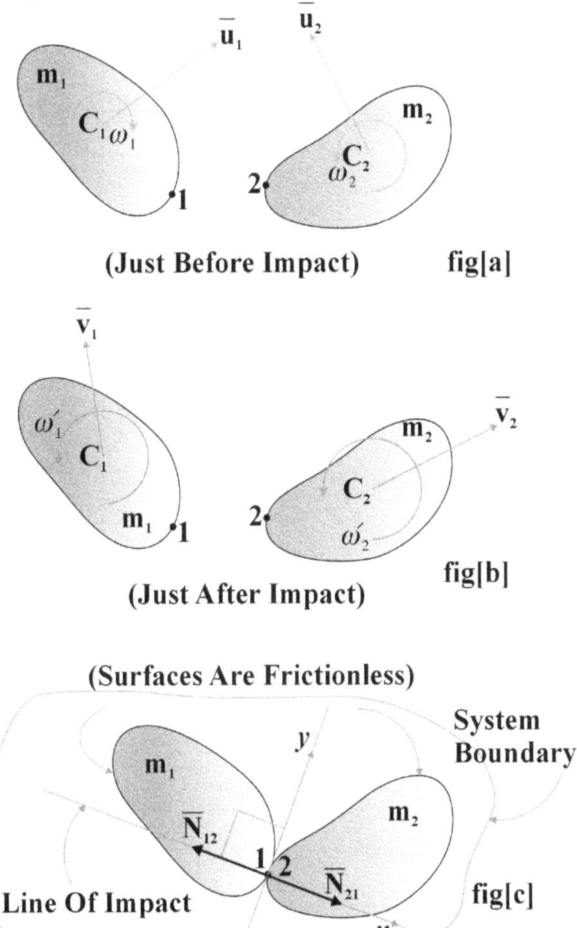

(Free Body Diagram During The Impact Period)

If both colliding bodies taken together as a single system as shown in the previous fig[c], and we simply assume that the all external forces acting on the system are negligible and body surfaces are frictionless; then the total linear momentum vector of the system will remain conserved. That is, referring the previous fig[a] and [b]:

$$\sum \vec{p}_{\left(\substack{\text{just before}\\\text{impact}}\right)} = \sum \vec{p}_{\left(\substack{\text{just after}\\\text{impact}}\right)} \rightarrow m_1\vec{u}_1 + m_2\vec{u}_2 = m_1\vec{v}_1 + m_2\vec{v}_2 - (i)$$

If the velocity vectors are coplanar, then they will have two orthogonal components, x and y. Then in component form:

$$m_1 u_{1x} + m_2 u_{2x} = m_1 v_{1x} + m_2 v_{2x} - (ii)$$

$$m_1 u_{1y} + m_2 u_{2y} = m_1 v_{1y} + m_2 v_{2y} - (iii)$$

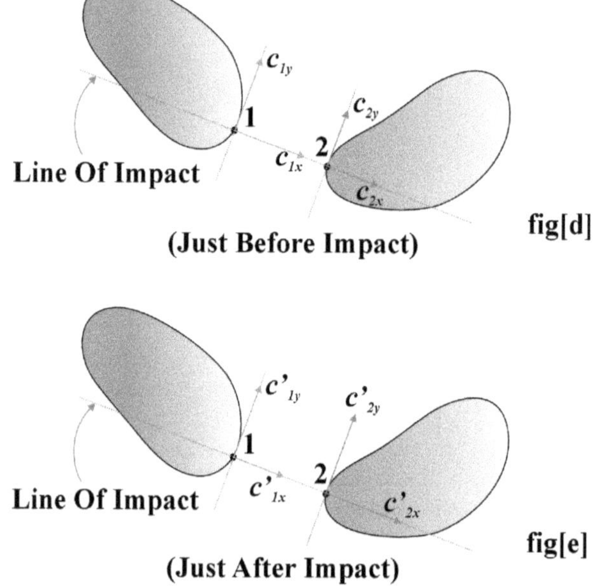

Similarly applying Newton's equation in the previous fig[d] & [e]:

$$\left|vel_{rec}\right|_{12} = e\left|vel_{app}\right|_{12} \rightarrow \left|c'_{2x} - c'_{1x}\right| = e\left|c_{1x} - c_{2x}\right| \quad -(iv)$$

Where points 1 & 2 are the actual points of contact during the collision.

$\left|vel_{rec}\right|_{12}$ = modulus of vel of recession between 1 and 2.

$\left|vel_{app}\right|_{12}$ = modulus of vel of approach between 1 and 2.

e = coefficient of restitution between points 1 and 2.

In this way using the equations (ii), (iii) and (iv), we can solve any three unknowns in the numerical problems.

3.4. EXPLOSION OF AN ORDINARY BOMB:

Suppose an ordinary bomb (not nuclear) of mass M is moving with velocity v at an angle θ with the horizontal as shown in the next figure. Suddenly it explodes into three pieces of mass m_1, m_2 and m_3 moving with velocities v_1, v_2 and v_3 respectively and also suppose that m_2 is moving horizontally. m_1 is moving at θ_1 with horizontal and m_3 is moving at θ_2 with horizontal as shown below. Also suppose that all external forces acting on the system are negligible as compared to the internal separating forces, hence the total linear momentum vector of the system will remain conserved.

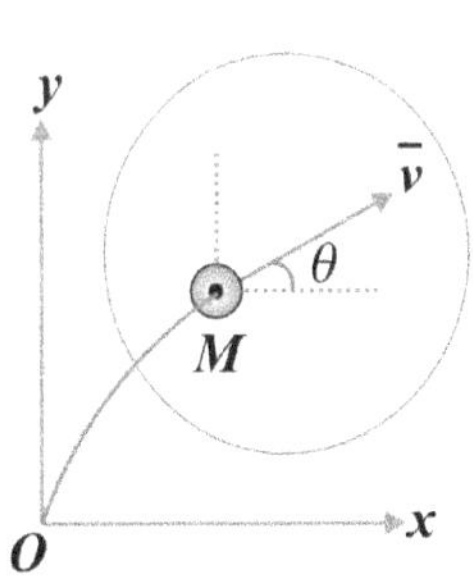

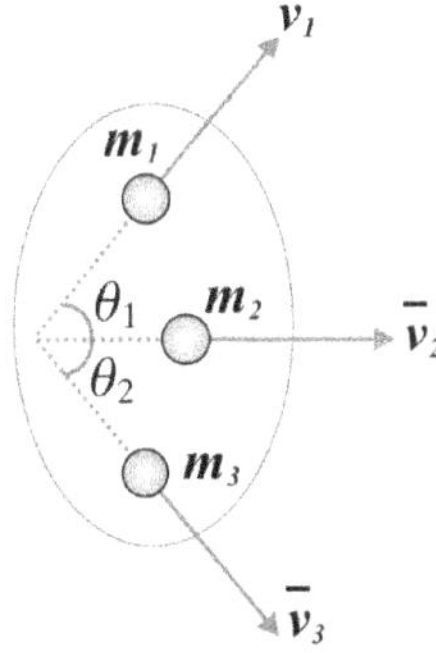

(Just Before Explosion)   (Just After Explosion)

Applying the principle of momentum conservation:

In vector form: $M\vec{v} = m_1\vec{v}_1 + m_2\vec{v}_2 + m_3\vec{v}_3$

In component form : Along x-axis :

$$Mv\cos\theta = m_1v_1\cos\theta_1 + m_2v_2 + m_3v_3\cos\theta_3 - (i)$$

Along y-axis :

$$Mv\sin\theta = m_1v_1\sin\theta_1 + 0 - m_3v_3\sin\theta_3 - (ii)$$

According to the principle of mass conservation:

$$M = m_1 + m_2 + m_3 - (iii) \qquad \frac{K_f}{K_i} = n >> 1 \quad - (iv)$$

During the explosion of a bomb, the final kinetic energy K_f increases many times as compared to the initial kinetic energy K_i of the system because chemical energy of the system gets converted into heat (random kinetic energy), light and sound energy.

3.5.IMPULSE Impulse vector has two types:

(i)Linear Impulse ($\vec{I}_l$)

(ii)Angular Impulse ($\vec{I}_a$)

3.5.1.Linear Impulse: There are many occasions in daily life when a large force is applied on a body for a short interval of time. For example: hitting a cricket-ball by a bat, a ping-pong ball by a stick, striking nail by a hammer, and collision between the two bodies etc.

In such cases, the product of the average impulsive force and the collision/contact time-interval is called the 'linear impulse' of the force.

Thus, the linear impulse given to a body is equal to the change in the linear momentum of the COM of the body during the collision/contact period.

Hence the unit of linear impulse is the same as that of the linear momentum, that is, the SI unit is kgms^{-1} or Ns and the CGS unit is gcms^{-1} or dyne second. Its dimensional formula is [**MLT^{-1}**].

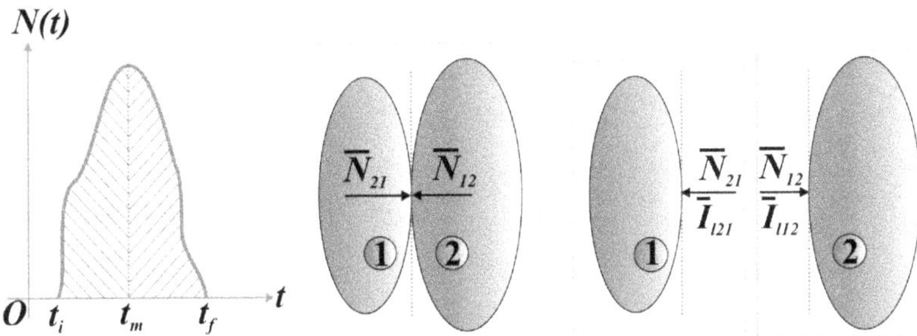

FBD of body 1 & 2   **FBD of body 1 & 2**

Fig (a)   **Fig (b)**   **Fig (c)**

During the impact as shown in the above fig (b), the colliding bodies 1 and 2 tend to deform each other by applying impulsive forces $\vec{N}_{12}$ and $\vec{N}_{21}$ as shown in the above figure (b) & (c). The magnitude of the impulsive force $\vec{N}_{12}$ and $\vec{N}_{21}$,or contact forces $\vec{N}_{12}$ and $\vec{N}_{21}$ that is, N is an absurd function of (t) time as shown in the previous graph (a). The magnitude of the impulsive contact force, that is, N first increases from zero, becomes maximum, then decreases to zero. Here $t=t_i$ to $t=t_m$ is called deformation time interval and $t=t_m$ to $t=t_f$ is called restoration time interval.

Here $\quad \vec{I}_{/12} = -\vec{I}_{/21}$ and $\vec{N}_{12} = -\vec{N}_{21}$

$\rightarrow |\vec{I}_{/12}| = |\vec{I}_{/21}| = I_{/}$ and $|\vec{N}_{12}| = |\vec{N}_{21}| = N$

t_i = the instant at which impact starts.

t_f = the instant at which impact gets over.

$\Delta t = t_f - t_i$ = collision time-interval or contact period

The area bounded by the N-t curve and t-axis gives us the magnitude of linear impulse by definition. Thus, we can say:

Statement 01: Linear Impulse imparted by the first body to the second body:

$$\vec{I}_{/12} = \int_{t_i}^{t_f} \vec{N}_{12}\,dt = \langle \vec{N}_{12} \rangle \Delta t = \Delta \vec{p}_{/12} = \begin{pmatrix} \text{Change in the linear mom-} \\ \text{entum of the second body} \end{pmatrix}$$

PROOF: By seeing the below known equations, we have:

We already know that total linear impulse imparted to the body-2 by the body-1 in the time interval (t_i to t_f):

$$\vec{I}_{l12} = \int_{t_i}^{t_f} \vec{N}_{12}\, dt = \left(\begin{array}{l} \text{Total area occupied by the graph} \left|\vec{N}_{12}\right| \\ vs\ t,\ \text{in the time interval } (t_i\ \text{to}\ t_f) \end{array} \right) - (i)$$

According to the Newton's second law:

$$\vec{N}_{12} = \frac{d\vec{p}_{l12}}{dt} \rightarrow \text{Then the average impulsive force:}$$

$$\left\langle \vec{N}_{12} \right\rangle = \frac{\Delta\vec{p}_{l12}}{\Delta t} \rightarrow \left\langle \vec{N}_{12} \right\rangle \Delta t = \Delta\vec{p}_{l12} - (ii)$$

From the eq(i): Total linear impulse imparted to the body-2 by the body-1 in the time interval (t_i to t_f):

$$\vec{I}_{l12} = \int_{t_i}^{t_f} \vec{N}_{12}\, dt = \int_{t_i}^{t_f} \frac{d\vec{p}_{l12}}{dt}\, dt \rightarrow \vec{I}_{l12} = \int_{t_i}^{t_f} d\vec{p}_{l12} = \left|\vec{p}_{l12}\right|_{\vec{p}_{l1}}^{\vec{p}_{l2}}$$

$$\rightarrow \vec{I}_{l12} = (\vec{p}_{l2} - \vec{p}_{l1}) \rightarrow \vec{I}_{l12} = \Delta\vec{p}_{l12} - (iii)$$

Now, from eq(i), (ii) and (iii), we have:

$$\vec{I}_{l12} = \int_{t_i}^{t_f} \vec{N}_{12}\, dt = \left\langle \vec{N}_{12} \right\rangle \Delta t = \Delta\vec{p}_{l12}$$

Statement 02: Linear Impulse imparted by the second body to the first body:

$$\vec{I}_{l21} = \int_{t_i}^{t_f} \vec{N}_{21}\, dt = \left\langle \vec{N}_{21} \right\rangle \Delta t = \Delta\vec{p}_{l21} = \left(\begin{array}{l} \text{Change in the linear mom-} \\ \text{entum of the first body} \end{array} \right)$$

PROOF: By seeing the below known equations, we have:

We already know that total linear impulse imparted to the body-1 by the body-2 in the time interval (t_i to t_f):

$$\vec{I}_{121} = \int_{t_i}^{t_f} \vec{N}_{21} dt = \left(\begin{array}{l} \text{Total area occupied by the graph} \left|\vec{N}_{21}\right| \\ vs\ t,\ \text{in the time interval } (t_i \text{ to } t_f) \end{array} \right) - (i)$$

According to the Newton's second law :

$$\vec{N}_{21} = \frac{d\vec{p}_{121}}{dt} \rightarrow \text{Then the average impulsive force:}$$

$$\left\langle \vec{N}_{21} \right\rangle = \frac{\Delta \vec{p}_{121}}{\Delta t} \rightarrow \left\langle \vec{N}_{21} \right\rangle \Delta t = \Delta \vec{p}_{121} - (ii)$$

From the eq(i) : Total linear impulse imparted to the body-1 by the body-2 in the time interval (t_i to t_f):

$$\vec{I}_{121} = \int_{t_i}^{t_f} \vec{N}_{21} dt = \int_{t_i}^{t_f} \frac{d\vec{p}_{121}}{dt} dt \rightarrow \vec{I}_{121} = \int_{t_i}^{t_f} d\vec{p}_{121} = \left|\vec{p}_{121}\right|_{\vec{p}_{l1}}^{\vec{p}_{l2}}$$

$$\rightarrow \vec{I}_{121} = (\vec{p}_{l2} - \vec{p}_{l1}) \rightarrow \vec{I}_{121} = \Delta \vec{p}_{121} - (iii)$$

Now, from eq(i), (ii) and (iii), we have : $\vec{I}_{121} = \int_{t_i}^{t_f} \vec{N}_{21} dt$

$$\rightarrow \vec{I}_{121} = \left\langle \vec{N}_{21} \right\rangle \Delta t = \Delta \vec{p}_{121}$$

Definition Of Coefficient Of Restitution (e):

Refer to the previous fig[a] on the page 30.
Coefficient of restitution (e) between the two points of contact :

$$e = \frac{\text{Area of restoration in the } N(t)\text{-}t \text{ graph}}{\text{Area of deformation in the } N(t)\text{-}t \text{ graph}} = \frac{\int_{t_m}^{t_f} N(t).dt}{\int_{t_i}^{t_m} N(t).dt} = \frac{\left|v_{recession}\right|}{\left|v_{approach}\right|}$$

3.5.2. Angular Impulse: There are many occasions in daily life when a large force is applied on a body for a short interval of time which produces an impulsive torque about a hinge. For example: hitting a hanging rigid bar by a fast moving ball or a bullet as shown in the next figure (b).

In such cases, the product of the average impulsive torque and the collision/contact time-interval is called the 'angular impulse' of the impulsive force.

Thus, the angular impulse given to a body about a hinge is equal to the change in the angular momentum of the body about the given hinge during the collision/contact period.

Hence, the unit of angular impulse is the same as that of the angular momentum, that is, the SI unit is Ns and the CGS unit is 'dyne second'. Its dimensional formula is $[ML^2T^{-1}]$.

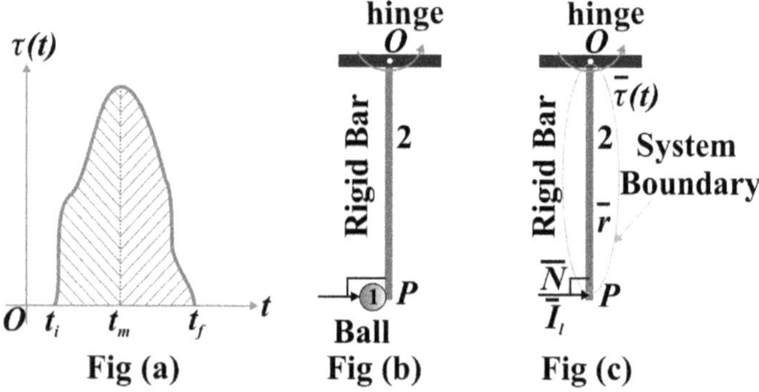

During the impact in the above fig (b), the ball 1 applies a large impulsive force $\vec{N}$ at point P of the rigid bar-2 as shown in the above fig (c). The impulsive force $\vec{N}$ produces an impulsive torque $\vec{\tau}(t)$ about the hinge O, which is an absurd function of time as shown in the above graph (a). The magnitude of impulsive torque $\vec{\tau}(t)$, that is, $\tau(t)$ first increases from zero, becomes maximum, then decreases to zero. Here, $t=t_i$ to $t=t_m$ is called deformation time interval and $t=t_m$ to $t=t_f$ is called restoration time interval.

Here the angular impulse imparted to the rigid bar-2 about the hinge O:

$\vec{I}_a = \vec{r} \times \vec{I}_l = $ Moment of the linear impulse (by definition) $- (i)$

Since $\quad \vec{I}_l = \langle \vec{N} \rangle \Delta t \rightarrow \vec{I}_a = \vec{r} \times \langle \vec{N} \rangle \Delta t = \langle \vec{\tau} \rangle \Delta t - (ii)$

Where $\langle \vec{\tau} \rangle = \vec{r} \times \langle \vec{N} \rangle = $ Moment of average impulsive force $\langle \vec{N} \rangle$

$\vec{r} = $ Position vector of the linear momentum of the COM of the ball about the hinge O.

$t_i = $ the initial instant at which impact starts

$t_f = $ the final instant at which impact gets over

$\Delta t = t_f - t_i = $ collision time $-$ interval or contact period

The area bounded by the τ-t curve and t-axis gives us the magnitude of angular impulse by definition. Thus, we can say: Angular Impulse imparted to the rigid bar-2 by the ball-1:

$$\vec{I}_a = \int_{t_i}^{t_f} \vec{\tau} dt = \langle \vec{\tau} \rangle \Delta t = \Delta \vec{L} = \left(\begin{array}{l} \text{Change in the angular momentum} \\ \text{of the rigid bar about the hinge } O. \end{array} \right) - (iii)$$

where $\Delta \vec{L} = \vec{L}_f - \vec{L}_i$

$\vec{L}_i = $ Initial ang. momentum of the rigid bar about the hinge O at $t = t_i$

$\vec{L}_f = $ Final ang. momentum of the rigid bar about the hinge O at $t = t_f$

Illustrations Of The Concept Of Linear Impulse:
(i) A cricketer moves his hands backwards while catching a ball.
(ii) A person jumping from a height on a pucca floor receives more injury than when jumping on a kuchcha floor.
(iii) Vehicles like cars, buses and scooters are provided with shockers.
(iv) Bogies of trains are provided with buffers.

4.0. NUMERICAL EXAMPLES

This section consists of two levels of mixed and solved question bank required for the development of understanding.

(i)Galaxy Level: JEE (main)/SAT Subject Test

(ii)Universal Level: IIT-JEE (adv)/KVPY/NTSE/Olympiads

EXAMPLE: For the two particle system, their masses and instantaneous position vectors are given as: m_1=2 kg, m_2=4 kg, $\vec{r}_1 = 2t^2\hat{i}$ m, $\vec{r}_2 = 4t^3\hat{j}$ m. For their centre of mass, find $\vec{r}_C, \vec{v}_C$ and $\vec{a}_C$ at t=1 sec .

SOLUTION: For the two-particle system, we already know:

$$\vec{r}_C(t) = \frac{m_1\vec{r}_1 + m_2\vec{r}_2}{m_1 + m_2} \rightarrow \vec{r}_C(t) = \frac{2(2t^2\hat{i}) + 4(4t^3\hat{j})}{2+4} = \frac{(2t^2\hat{i}) + (8t^3\hat{j})}{3}$$

$$\text{At } t = 1\sec, \ \vec{r}_C(1) = \frac{(2.1^2\hat{i}) + (8.1^3\hat{j})}{3} = \frac{2}{3}(\hat{i} + 4\hat{j}) \ m \quad \text{ANS}$$

$$\vec{v}_C(t) = \frac{d\vec{r}_C(t)}{dt} = \frac{d}{dt}\left(\frac{(2t^2\hat{i}) + (8t^3\hat{j})}{3}\right) = \frac{1}{3}\frac{d}{dt}\left((2t^2\hat{i}) + (8t^3\hat{j})\right)$$

$$\rightarrow \vec{v}_C(t) = (1/3)\left((4t\hat{i}) + (24t^2\hat{j})\right) \rightarrow \vec{v}_C(1) = \frac{4}{3}\left(\hat{i} + 6\hat{j}\right)ms^{-1} \quad \text{ANS}$$

$$\vec{a}_C(t) = \frac{d\vec{v}_C(t)}{dt} = \frac{d}{dt}\left(\frac{4}{3}\left(\hat{i} + 6t^2\hat{j}\right)\right) = \frac{4}{3}\frac{d}{dt}\left(t\hat{i} + 6t^2\hat{j}\right)$$

$$\rightarrow \vec{a}_C(t) = \frac{4}{3}\left(\hat{i} + 12t\hat{j}\right) \rightarrow \vec{a}_C(1) = \frac{4}{3}\left(\hat{i} + 12.1\hat{j}\right)$$

$$\rightarrow \vec{a}_C(1) = \frac{4}{3}\left(\hat{i} + 12\hat{j}\right) \ ms^{-2} \quad \text{ANS}$$

EXAMPLE: In the next fig (a), three uniform laminar bodies namely square lamina, half disc and triangular lamina are touching each other as shown. Given that m_1=2kg, m_2=6kg, m_3=10kg, a=2m, b=3m. For the given system, find out the coordinates of COM of the whole system.

SOLUTION: In the below fig (b), first we will locate the COM of each bodies separately and find out their coordinates $(x_1,y_1),(x_2,y_2)$ and (x_3,y_3). Suppose the COM of each bodies be represented as $C_1(x_1,y_1)$, $C_2(x_2,y_2)$ and $C_3(x_3,y_3)$ respectively.

$$x_1 = \frac{a}{2} = \frac{2}{2}m = 1m; \quad y_1 = \frac{a}{2} = \frac{2}{2}m = 1m,$$

$$x_2 = a + \frac{4r}{3\pi} = 2 + \frac{4(2/2)}{3\pi} = \left(2 + \frac{4}{3\pi}\right)m, \; y_2 = \frac{a}{2} = \frac{2}{2}m = 1m$$

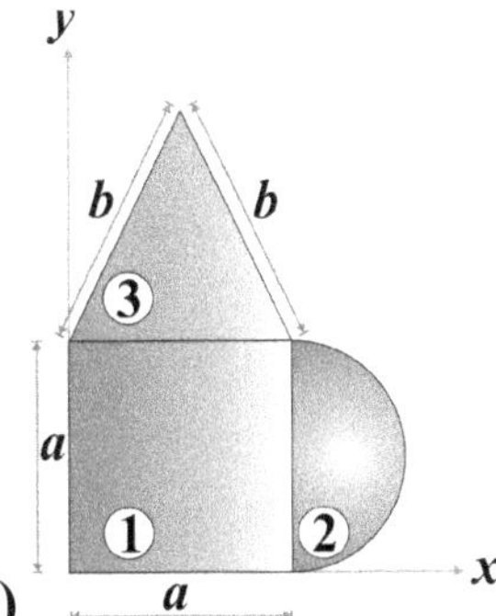

We can simply realise that : $x_3 = \dfrac{a}{2} = \dfrac{2}{2}m = 1m$, $y_3 = \left(a + \dfrac{h}{3}\right)$;

where $h = \sqrt{b^2 - \left(\dfrac{a}{2}\right)^2} = \sqrt{b^2 - \left(\dfrac{a}{2}\right)^2} = \sqrt{3^2 - \left(\dfrac{2}{2}\right)^2} = \sqrt{8}\ m$

$\rightarrow y_3 = \left(2 + \dfrac{\sqrt{8}}{3}\right)\ m$; we know $x_C = \dfrac{m_1 x_1 + m_2 x_2 + m_3 x_3}{m_1 + m_2 + m_3}$

$\rightarrow x_C = \dfrac{2 \times 1 + 6 \times \left(2 + \dfrac{4}{3\pi}\right) + 10 \times 1}{2 + 6 + 10}\, m = \dfrac{24 + \dfrac{8}{\pi}}{18}\, m = \left(\dfrac{4}{3} + \dfrac{4}{9\pi}\right)m$

$$\rightarrow y_C = \frac{2\times1 + 6\times1 + 10\times\left(2 + \frac{\sqrt{8}}{3}\right)}{2 + 6 + 10}\, m \rightarrow y_C = \frac{28 + \frac{10\sqrt{8}}{3}}{18}\, m$$

$$\rightarrow y_C = \left(\frac{14}{9} + \frac{10\sqrt{2}}{27}\right)m \qquad\qquad \text{ANS}$$

EXAMPLE: In the adjacent fig, there is a uniform disc of

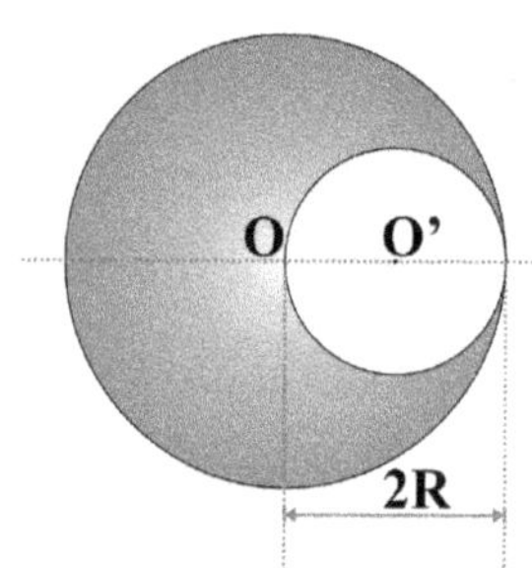

radius 2R. Another small disc of radius R (centre at O') has been cut and removed as shown. For the remaining disc, find the distance of its COM from point O.

SOLUTION: Suppose the uniform mass density of the solid portion of the given disc is σ kg/m^2. Now, consider uncut body, cut portion and the remaining body as shown below. We can simply realise that the mass distribution is symmetrical about the shown x-axis. Hence, the position of COM in each case will be situated on the x-axis itself as shown below.

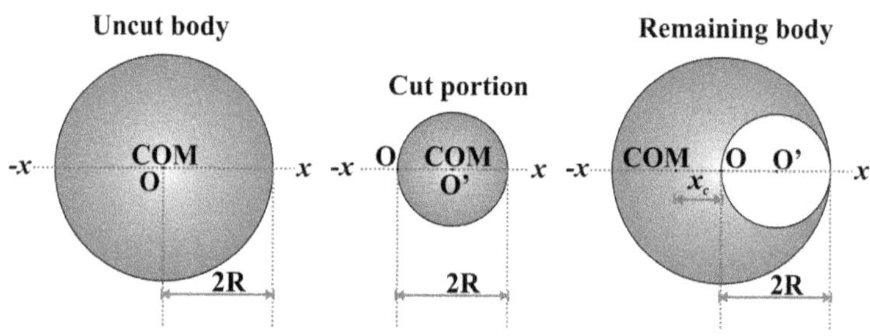

For the uncut body, $x_{uncut}=0$. For the cut portion, $x_{cut}=+R$. For the remaining body, suppose it is given: $x_{res}=x_c$ (unknown)

$$x_{res} = x_c = \frac{m_{uncut}\, x_{uncut} - m_{cut} x_{cut}}{m_{uncut} - m_{cut}} = \frac{\sigma\pi(2R)^2(0) - \sigma\pi(R)^2(+R)}{\sigma\pi(2R)^2 - \sigma\pi(R)^2}$$

$$\to x_c = -\frac{R}{3} \to |x_c| = \frac{R}{3} \qquad \text{ANS}$$

EXAMPLE: In the below figure, we are given a non-uniform bar of length L with linear mass density $\lambda=kx^2$, then locate the position of its COM.

$$\lambda = kx^2$$

$$O \quad x=0 \qquad\qquad\qquad x=L \qquad x$$

SOLUTION: We already know that for a continuum system, the x-coordinate of its COM:(See the below fig for the ref.)

$$\lambda = kx^2 \quad dx$$

$$O \quad x=0 \qquad dm \qquad\qquad x=L \qquad x$$

$$x_{CM} = \frac{\Sigma(m_i x_i)}{\Sigma(m_i)} = \frac{\int (dm)x}{\int (dm)} \quad -(i)$$

We also know that the linear mass density : $\lambda = \dfrac{dm}{dx} = kx^2$

$$\to dm = kx^2 dx \to x_{CM} = \frac{\int (dm)x}{\int (dm)} = \frac{\displaystyle\int_{x=0}^{x=L} (kx^2\,dx)\,x}{\displaystyle\int_{x=0}^{x=L} (kx^2\,dx)} , \left(\text{From eq}(i)\right)$$

$$x_{CM} = \frac{\int\limits_{x=0}^{x=L}\left(kx^3 dx\right)}{\int\limits_{x=0}^{x=L}\left(kx^2 dx\right)} = \frac{\int\limits_{x=0}^{x=L}\left(x^3 dx\right)}{\int\limits_{x=0}^{x=L}\left(x^2 dx\right)} = \frac{\left.\dfrac{x^4}{4}\right|_0^L}{\left.\dfrac{x^3}{3}\right|_0^L} = \frac{3}{4}\frac{L^4 - 0^4}{L^3 - 0^3} = \frac{3}{4}L; \ \text{ANS}$$

EXAMPLE: In the adjacent fig, we are given a non-uniform half disc of radius R whose surface mass density $\sigma = kr^3$, where $k>0$ constant. Locate its COM.

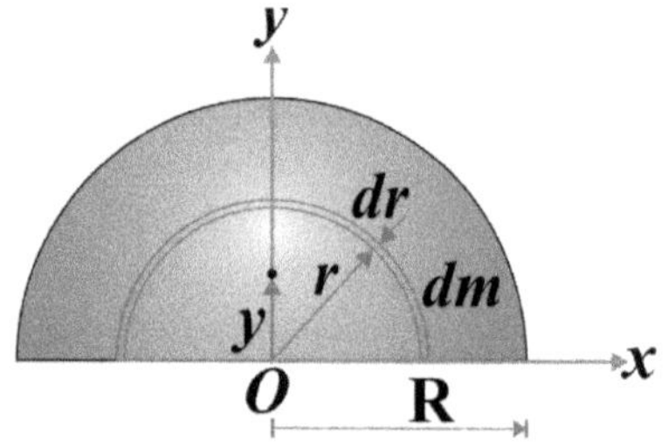

SOLUTION: We can simply realise that y-axis is the axis of symmetry, hence the COM must be located on the y-axis itself. Consider a very thin half ring element of radius r and thickness dr and mass dm as shown in the above figure. We know that for a continuum system:

$$y_{CM} = \frac{\Sigma(m_i y_i)}{\Sigma(m_i)} = \frac{\int (dm)y}{\int (dm)} - (i) \quad \begin{pmatrix} \textit{Where y is the y}-\textit{coordinate of the} \\ \textit{COM of the half ring element of} \\ \textit{radius r.That is}: y = 2r/\pi. \textit{ We also} \\ \textit{know that the surface mass density}: \end{pmatrix}$$

$$\sigma = \frac{dm}{dA} = kr^3 \ \ (\text{Given}) \rightarrow dm = kr^3 dA = kr^3 \pi r dr,$$

$$\text{where } dA = \begin{pmatrix} \text{Surface area of the} \\ \text{half ring element} \end{pmatrix} = \pi r dr$$

$$\rightarrow y_{CM} = \frac{\int (dm)y}{\int (dm)} = \frac{\int\limits_{r=0}^{r=R}\left(kr^3 \pi r dr\right)(2r/\pi)}{\int\limits_{r=0}^{r=R}\left(kr^3 \pi r dr\right)} = \frac{2\int\limits_{r=0}^{r=R}\left(r^5 dr\right)}{\pi \int\limits_{r=0}^{r=R}\left(r^4 dr\right)}, \begin{pmatrix} \text{From} \\ \text{eq } (i) \end{pmatrix}$$

$$\to y_{CM} = \frac{2}{\pi} \frac{\left. \left| r^6/6 \right| \right._0^R}{\left. \left| r^5/5 \right| \right._0^R} = \frac{2}{\pi} \frac{5}{6} \frac{R^6 - 0^6}{R^5 - 0^5} = \frac{5R}{3\pi} \qquad \text{ANS}$$

EXAMPLE: In the below fig, we are given a non-uniform hemi-sphere of radius R whose volume mass density $\rho = kr$, where $k>0$ constant. Locate its COM.

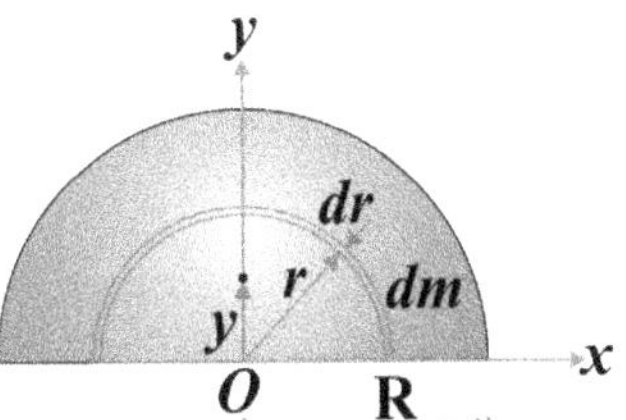

SOLUTION: We can simply realise that y-axis is the axis of symmetry, hence the COM must be located on the y-axis itself. Consider a very thin hemi-sphere element of radius r, thickness dr and mass dm as shown in the above figure. We know that for a continuum system:

$$y_{CM} = \frac{\Sigma\left(m_i y_i\right)}{\Sigma\left(m_i\right)} = \frac{\int\left(dm\right)y}{\int\left(dm\right)} \quad -(i)$$

Where y is the y-coordinate of the COM of the hemi-sphere element of radius r. That is: $y=r/2$. We also know that the volume mass density:

$$\rho = \frac{dm}{dV} = kr \ \ (\text{Given}) \to dm = krdV = kr2\pi r^2 dr,$$

where $dV = \left(\text{Volume of the hemi-sphere element}\right) = 2\pi r^2 dr$

$$\to y_{CM} = \frac{\int\left(dm\right)y}{\int\left(dm\right)} = \frac{\displaystyle\int_{r=0}^{r=R}\left(kr2\pi r^2 dr\right)(r/2)}{\displaystyle\int_{r=0}^{r=R}\left(kr2\pi r^2 dr\right)} = \frac{\displaystyle\int_{r=0}^{r=R}\left(r^4 dr\right)}{2\displaystyle\int_{r=0}^{r=R}\left(r^3 dr\right)}, \left(\begin{array}{c}\text{From}\\ \text{eq }(i)\end{array}\right)$$

$$\rightarrow y_{CM} = \frac{1}{2}\frac{\left|r^5/5\right|_0^R}{\left|r^4/4\right|_0^R} = \frac{1}{2}\frac{4}{5}\frac{R^5-0^5}{R^4-0^4} = \frac{2}{5}R \qquad \text{ANS}$$

EXAMPLE: In the below fig, there is a stationary boat of length L and mass M standing in a lake along with a small dog (zero size) at point A. When the dog runs from A to B, the boat displaces by d to the left. Ignoring water friction, find out the value of d.

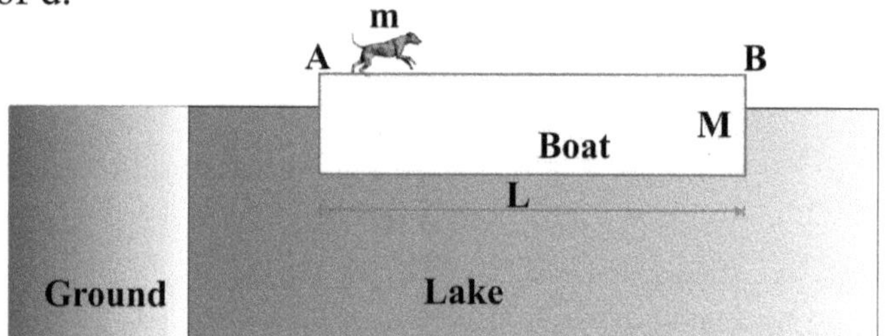

SOLUTION: **METHOD 01:** See the previous fig (a). Suppose at t=0, the dog is standing at point A. Then the dog starts running rightwards and reaches the point B at t=T. In this time interval, the boat recoils back due to the friction between the dog feet and the boat top surface. Suppose the backward displacement of the boat is d as shown in the fig (b), with respect to the ground frame or the stationary inertial frame.

From the fig (a) and the fig (b), we can simply analyse that the net rightward displacement of the dog will be (L-d), with respect to stationary inertial frame. If we consider the boat and the dog as a single system then there is no external horizontal force acting on the system boundary because the water resistance is given as zero. We have already proved that:

If $\left(F_{ext}\right)_x = 0$ and initial $\left(p_{CM}\right)_x = 0$, then between $t = 0$ & $t = T$:

$$m_1\Delta x_1 + m_2\Delta x_2 + m_3\Delta x_3 + ... + m_N\Delta x_N = 0; \text{ [wrt inertial frame]}$$

where Δx_1 = horizontal displacement of the COM of the 1st body

Δx_2 = horizontal displacement of the COM of the 2nd body

Δx_N = horizontal displacement of the COM of the Nth body

For the two body system : $m_1 \Delta x_1 + m_2 \Delta x_2 = 0 - (i)$
If m_1=m and m_2=M, then:
Δx_1=+(L-d)=[rightward displacement of the dog]
and Δx_2=-d=[leftward displacement of the boat]
  Here, we will make a sign convention for our own; that is, the rightward vectors are +ve and the leftward vectors are -ve. Putting these values in eq (i), we have:

$$m\left[+(L-d)\right]+M\left[-d\right]=0 \rightarrow d(m+M)=mL$$

$$\rightarrow d = \frac{mL}{(m+M)} \quad \text{ANS}$$

METHOD 02: See the next fig (c) for the reference. As the dog runs from point (A) to the point (B) in time interval t=0 to t=T, the actual displacement of the boat wrt IF: Δx_B=-d $-(i)$

  The relative displacement of the dog with respect to the boat or with respect to the non-inertial frame fixed to the boat: Δx_{DB}=+L $-(ii)$

  By definition, we know: Δx_{DB}=Δx_D-Δx_B
$\rightarrow \Delta x_D$=Δx_{DB}+Δx_B
$\rightarrow \Delta x_D$=[+L]+[-d]$\rightarrow \Delta x_D$=(L-d) $-(iii)$

But we have already proved that :

If $\left(F_{ext}\right)_x = 0$ and initial $(p_{CM})_x = 0$, then between $t = 0$ & $t = T$:

$m_1 \Delta x_1 + m_2 \Delta x_2 = 0 \rightarrow m_D \Delta x_D + m_B \Delta x_B = 0 - (iv)$

[wrt inertial frame]

From eq$(i),(iii)$ & (iv) we have : m[+(L-d)]+M[-d] = 0

$$\rightarrow d(m+M) = mL \rightarrow d = \frac{mL}{(m+M)} \quad \text{ANS}$$

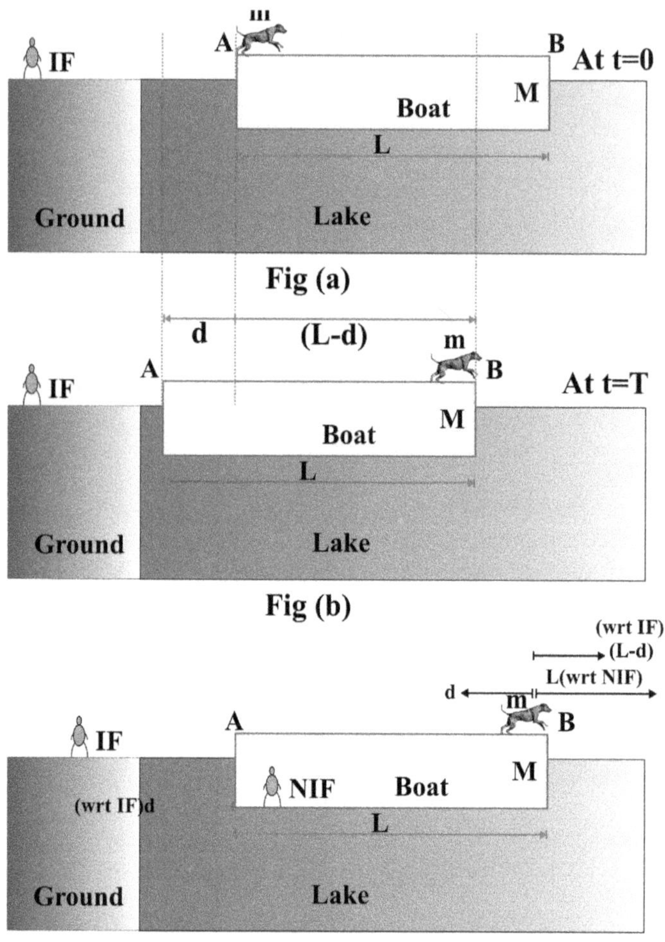

EXAMPLE: In the next fig (a), there is a big block of the mass M with hemicylindrical cavity placed on a fixed table as shown. A small sphere of the mass m is released from rest at point A as shown. When the sphere reaches point B, then find out the displacement of the big block in ground frame. Friction is zero everywhere.

SOLUTION: METHOD 01: See the next fig (b). Suppose at

t=0, the ball is released at point A. Then the ball starts sliding rightwards and reaches the point B at t=T. In this time interval, the big block recoils back due to the reaction force between the ball and the big block. Suppose the backward displacement of the big block is d as shown in the next fig (c), with respect to the ground frame or the stationary inertial frame. From the next fig (b) and the fig (c), we can simply analyse that the net rightward displacement of the ball will be (R-r-d), with respect to stationary inertial frame.

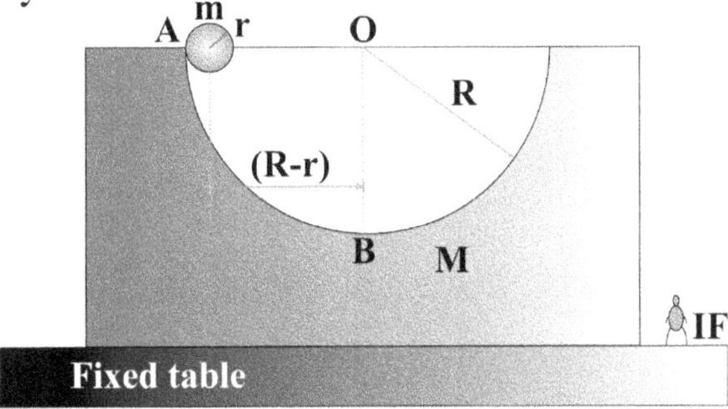

Fig (a)

If we consider the big block and the ball as a single system then there is no external horizontal force acting on the system boundary because the surface friction is given as zero. We have already proved that:

If $\left(F_{ext}\right)_x = 0$ and initial $\left(p_{CM}\right)_x = 0$, then between $t = 0$ & $t = T$:

$m_1\Delta x_1 + m_2\Delta x_2 + m_3\Delta x_3 + ... + m_N\Delta x_N = 0$; [wrt inertial frame]

Δx_1 = horizontal displacement of the COM of the 1st body

Δx_2 = horizontal displacement of the COM of the 2nd body

....

Δx_N = horizontal displacement of the COM of the Nth body

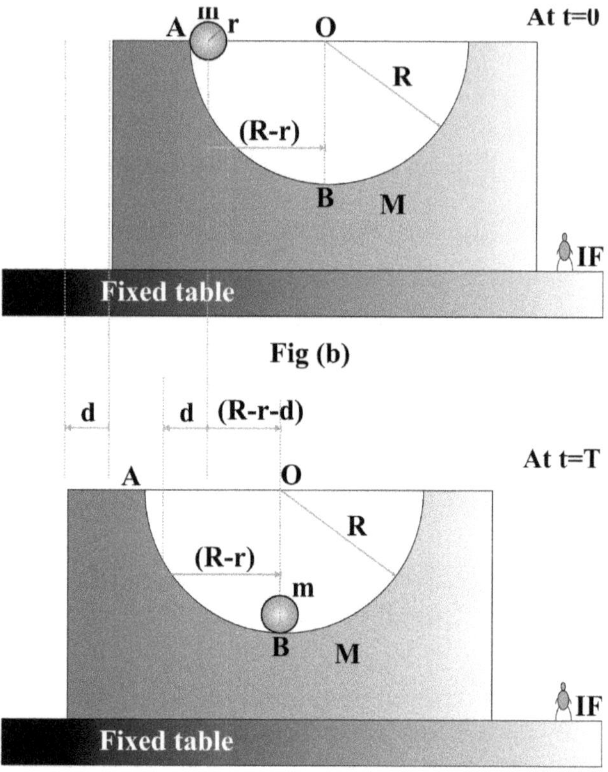

Fig (c)

For the two body system : $m_1 \Delta x_1 + m_2 \Delta x_2 = 0 - (i)$

If m_1=m and m_2=M, then:

Δx_1=+(R-r-d)=[rightward displacement of the ball]

and Δx_2=-d=[leftward displacement of the big block]

Here, we will make a sign convention for our own; that is, the rightward vectors are +ve and the leftward vectors are -ve. Putting these values in eq (*i*), we have:

$$m\left[+(R-r-d)\right]+M\left[-d\right]=0 \rightarrow d(m+M)=m(R-r)$$

$$\rightarrow d = \frac{m(R-r)}{(m+M)} \text{ ANS}$$

METHOD 02: See the next fig (d) for reference. As the ball

slides from point (A) to the point (B) in time interval t=0 to t=T, the actual displacement of the big block wrt IF:
Δx_B=-d –(*i*)

The relative displacement of the ball with respect to the big block or with respect to the non-inertial frame fixed to the big block: Δx_{bB}=+(R-r) –(*ii*)   By definition, we know:
Δx_{bB}=Δx_b-Δx_B →Δx_b=Δx_{bB}+Δx_B, Δx_b=[+(R-r)]+[-d]
→ Δx_b=(R-r-d) –(*iii*)

Fig (d)

But we have already proved that :

If $\left(F_{ext}\right)_x = 0$ and initial $(p_{CM})_x = 0,$ then between t = 0 & t = T:

$m_1\Delta x_1 + m_2\Delta x_2 = 0$; [wrt inertial frame]

$\rightarrow m_b\Delta x_b + m_B\Delta x_B = 0 - (iv)$

From eq$(i),(iii)$ & (iv) we have : m[+(R-r-d)]+M[-d] = 0

$$\rightarrow d(m+M) = m(R-r) \rightarrow d = \frac{m(R-r)}{(m+M)} \quad \text{ANS}$$

EXAMPLE: In the next figure, a block of mass M is connected to a small ring of mass m and held in horizontal position as shown. Now, the system is released from rest. The

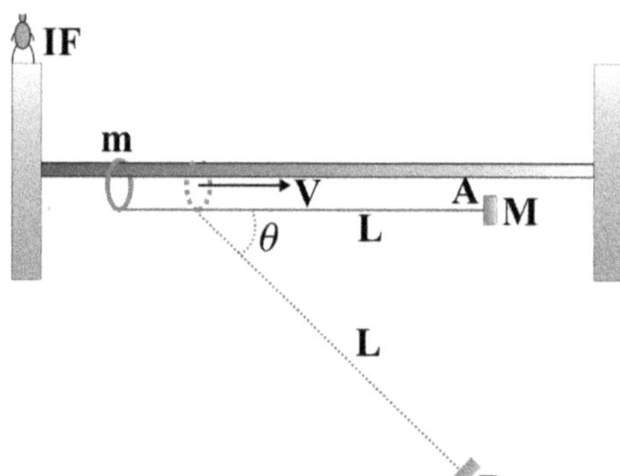

ring of mass m starts sliding over the rigid frictionless rod as shown. When the string of length L makes an angle θ with the horizontal direction then find out the displacement d of the ring in ground frame or stationary inertial frame.

SOLUTION: See the next fig (a) and (b) for the reference. As the ring slides rightward in time interval t=0 to t=T, the actual displacement of the ring wrt IF:

$\Delta x_R = +d$ —(i)

The relative horizontal displacement of the block with respect to the ring or with respect to the non-inertial frame fixed to the ring: $\Delta x_{BR} = -(L - L\cos\theta)$ —(ii)

By definition, we know:

$\Delta x_{BR} = \Delta x_B - \Delta x_R \rightarrow \Delta x_B = \Delta x_{BR} + \Delta x_R$

$\rightarrow \Delta x_B = [-(L - L\cos\theta)] + [+d] \rightarrow \Delta x_B = [d - (L - L\cos\theta)]$ —(iii)

But we have already proved that :

If $\left(F_{ext}\right)_x = 0$ and initial $(p_{CM})_x = 0$, then between $t = 0$ & $t = T$:

$m_1\Delta x_1 + m_2\Delta x_2 = 0$; [wrt inertial frame]

$\rightarrow m_R\Delta x_R + m_B\Delta x_B = 0$ —(iv)

From eq(i), (iii) & (iv) we have : $m[+d] + M[-(L - L\cos\theta - d)] = 0$

$\rightarrow d(m+M) = M(L - L\cos\theta) \rightarrow d = \dfrac{ML(1-\cos\theta)}{(m+M)}$ ANS

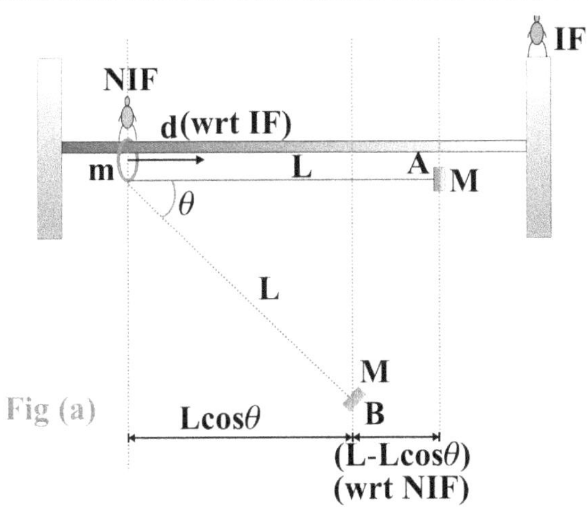

EXAMPLE: In the below fig, there is a designer block of mass M, whose BC part is vertical quarter circular of radius h and AB part is horizontal plane. This is placed over fixed and frictionless plane as shown. A very small block of mass m is released at point A with velocity u as shown. Find out the velocity of the designer block at the moment when the small block breaks off at point C. Also find out the break off velocity of the small block in ground frame as well as in a frame fixed to the designer block. Friction is zero everywhere.

SOLUTION: See the next fig (a) for FBD of the system. On the system boundary, external forces acting are only **N** and **(M+m)g**. No external horizontal force is acting on the system. It means

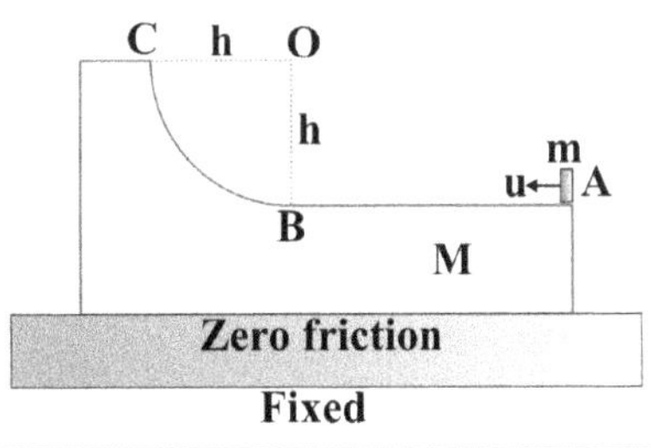

$\sum F_x=0 \rightarrow p_{cx}$=constant at every moment.

Let us make a sign convention. Suppose leftward vector is positive and rightward vector is negative.

See the next fig (b) for reference. At t=0, the initial horizontal momentum of the COM: $\quad p_{cxi}=p_m+p_M=mu+M(0)$

$\rightarrow p_{cxi}=mu -(i)$

See the next fig (c) for reference. At t=T, the relative velocity of m wrt M or wrt NIF fixed to M; will be v_y (upward) as shown. Suppose at this moment M acquires velocity V (leftward wrt IF) as shown. That is:

$$\vec{v}_M = \vec{V},\ \vec{v}_{mM} = \vec{v}_y \text{ but } \vec{v}_{mM} = \vec{v}_m - \vec{v}_M \rightarrow \vec{v}_m = \vec{v}_{mM} + \vec{v}_M$$

$$\rightarrow \vec{v}_m = \vec{v}_y + \vec{V} = \text{Actual vel of small block wrt IF or ground frame}$$

$$\rightarrow |\vec{v}_m| = v_{net} = \sqrt{\left|\vec{v}_y\right|^2 + \left|\vec{V}\right|^2} \rightarrow v_m = v_{net} = \sqrt{v_y^2 + V^2} - (ii)$$

In next fig (c) at t=T,

The final horizontal momentum of the COM:

$p_{cxf}=p_m+p_M=mV+MV$

$\rightarrow p_{cxf}=V(m+M) -(iii)$

According to the principle of momentum conservation:

$p_{cxi}=p_{cxf} \rightarrow mu=V(m+M)$ [From eq(i) and eq(iii)]

$$\rightarrow V = \frac{mu}{m+M}$$

$\rightarrow V$ = Vel of M wrt IF or ground frame   ANS

Since $\Delta W_{inc}=0$ and $\Delta W_{enc}=0$, hence the total mechanical energy of the system will remain conserved. That is in time interval t=0 to t=T:

The loss in kinetic energy wrt IF=The gain in gravitational potential energy wrt IF:

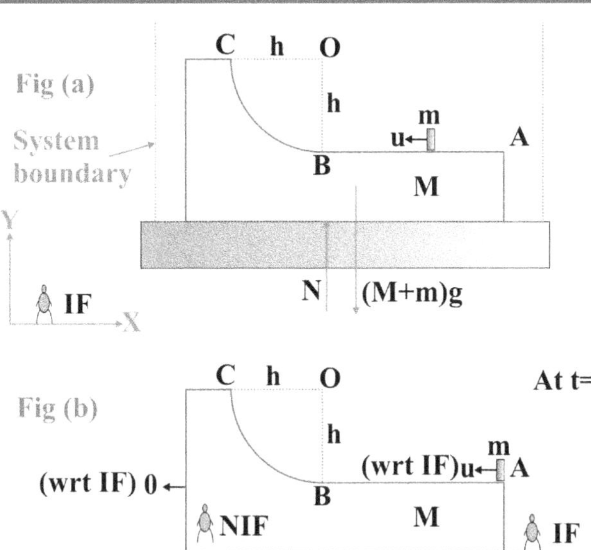

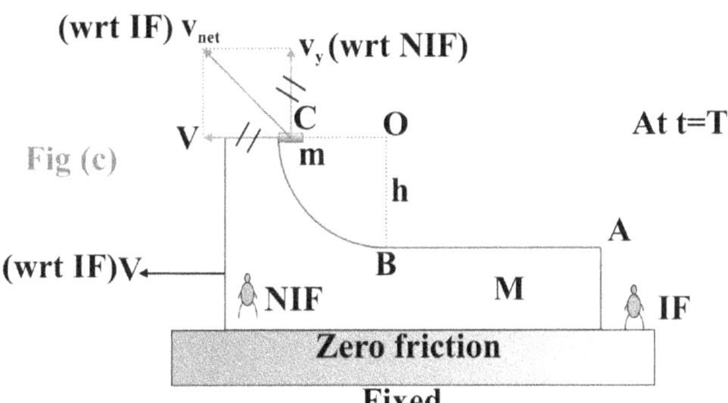

$$\to \frac{1}{2}mu^2 - \left(\frac{1}{2}MV^2 + \frac{1}{2}mv_m^2\right) = mgh + 0$$

$$\to mu^2 - MV^2 - m\left(\sqrt{v_y^2 + V^2}\right)^2 = 2mgh, \begin{pmatrix} \text{by putting the} \\ \text{value of } v_m \end{pmatrix}$$

$$\rightarrow mu^2 - (M+m)\left(\frac{mu}{m+M}\right)^2 - mv_y^2 = 2mgh, \begin{pmatrix} \text{by putting the} \\ \text{value of V} \end{pmatrix}$$

$$\rightarrow u^2\left(1 - \frac{m}{M+m}\right) - 2gh = v_y^2 \rightarrow v_y = \sqrt{u^2\left(\frac{M}{M+m}\right) - 2gh} \quad \text{ANS}$$

v_y is the relative vel of m wrt M or wrt NIF fixed to M.

$$\rightarrow v_m = v_{net} = \sqrt{v_y^2 + V^2} = \sqrt{u^2\left(\frac{M}{M+m}\right) - 2gh + \left(\frac{mu}{m+M}\right)^2}$$

$$\rightarrow v_m = \sqrt{\left(\frac{Mu^2}{M+m}\right) - 2gh + \left(\frac{mu}{m+M}\right)^2} \quad \text{ANS}$$

v_m is the actual vel of m wrt ground frame or IF.

EXAMPLE: In the next shown fig (a), a small ring of mass m and a block of mass M are tied with a massless inextensible string of length L and held in horizontal position as shown. The ring can slide over a rigid fixed horizontal frictionless rod. At t=0, the system is released from rest. Find the velocity V of the ring in ground frame when the string makes an angle θ with the horizontal.

SOLUTION: Consider m (ring), M (block) and the connecting string as a system. See the FBD of the system in fig (b). The only external forces acting on the system are N and (m+M)g. There is no external horizontal force acting on the system. That is: $\qquad \sum F_x = 0 \rightarrow p_{cx} = $ constant

At t=0, in horizontal position, $p_{cxi} = 0$ $-(i)$

See the next Fig (a) for reference. Suppose at t=T, the string makes angle θ with horizontal and the ring acquires vel V wrt IF as shown. If we fix a frame to the moving ring then this will be called NIF. With respect to NIF the ring will be perceived in relative rest as shown in next fig (a).

With respect to NIF, the block M will be perceived as moving along a circular trajectory of radius L.

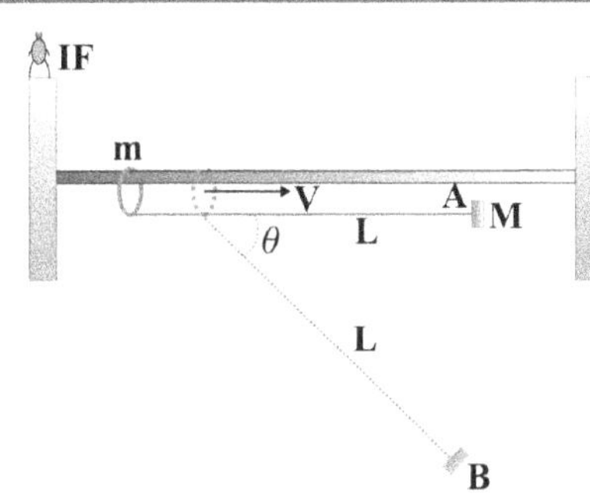

Suppose at t=T, the tangential relative vel of M is v in NIF. That is:

We also know that :

$$\vec{v}_{BR} = \vec{v}_B - \vec{v}_R \rightarrow \vec{v}_B$$

$$\rightarrow \vec{v}_{BR} + \vec{v}_R = \vec{v}_{net}$$

$$\rightarrow \vec{v}_B = \vec{v}_{net} = \vec{v} + \vec{V};$$

[From eq (ii) and (iii)]

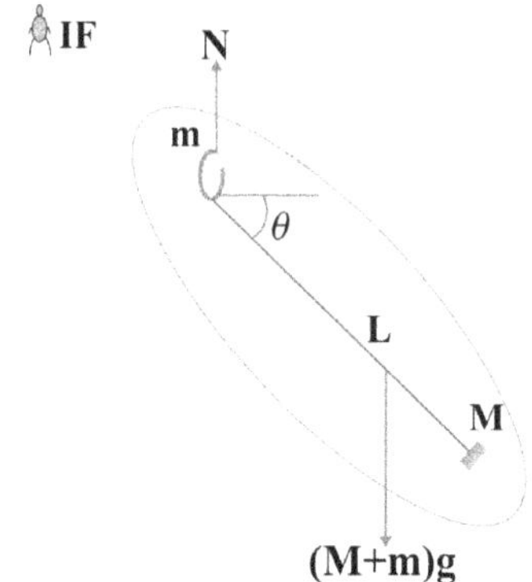

According to the parallelogram law:[from the above fig (b)]

$$\left|\vec{v}_B\right| = \left|\vec{v}_{net}\right| = \sqrt{v^2 + V^2 + 2vV\cos(90+\theta)} = \sqrt{v^2 + V^2 - 2vV\sin\theta}$$

$$\rightarrow \left|\vec{v}_B\right| = \left|\vec{v}_{net}\right| = \sqrt{v^2 + V^2 - 2vV\sin\theta} - (iv)$$

At t=T, the final horizontal momentum of the system:

$p_{cxf}=p_{xR}+p_{xB}=[+mV]+[+M(V-v\sin\theta)] -(v)$

[see the previous fig (a) & (b)], since p_{cx}=constant$\rightarrow p_{cxi}= p_{cxf}$

$\rightarrow 0=[+mV]+[+M(V-v\sin\theta)]$; [from eq ($i$) & ($v$)]

$\rightarrow (m+M)V= Mv\sin\theta \rightarrow V= Mv\sin\theta/(m+M) -(vi)$

Also, we can analyse that for the system shown, in t=0 to t=T:

ΔW_{inc}=The work done by internal non conservative forces=0

ΔW_{enc}=The work done by external non conservative forces=0

Hence the total mechanical energy of the system will remain conserved. That is, in inertial frame of reference:

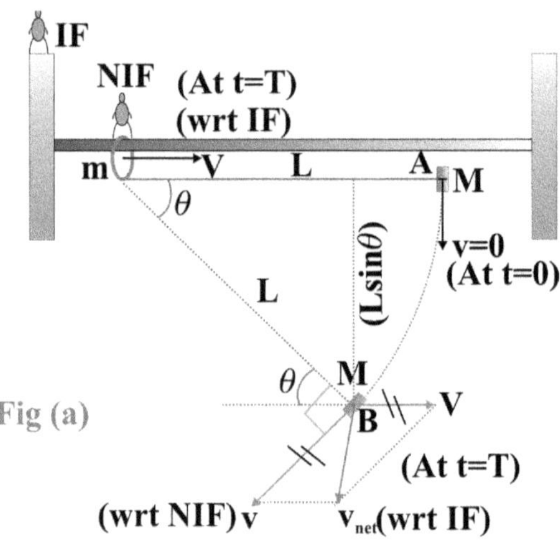

The loss in total gravitational potential energy =The gain in total kinetic energy. [See the below from eq(vi)]

$$\rightarrow MgLsin\theta = \frac{1}{2}mV^2 + \frac{1}{2}Mv_{net}^2 \rightarrow 2MgLsin\theta = mV^2 + Mv_{net}^2$$

$$\rightarrow 2MgLsin\theta = mV^2 + M\left(v^2 + V^2 - 2vVsin\theta\right)$$

$$\rightarrow 2MgLsin\theta = (m+M)V^2 + Mv^2 - 2MvVsin\theta$$

$$\rightarrow 2MgLsin\theta = (m+M)\left(\frac{Mvsin\theta}{m+M}\right)^2 + Mv^2 - 2Mv\left(\frac{Mvsin\theta}{m+M}\right)sin\theta$$

$$\rightarrow 2MgLsin\theta = v^2\left[M - \frac{M^2sin^2\theta}{m+M}\right]$$

$$\rightarrow 2MgLsin\theta = v^2\left[\frac{Mm+M^2-M^2sin^2\theta}{m+M}\right]$$

$$\rightarrow 2gLsin\theta = v^2\left[\frac{m+Mcos^2\theta}{m+M}\right] \rightarrow v = \sqrt{\frac{2gL(m+M)sin\theta}{m+Mcos^2\theta}} - (vii)$$

$$\rightarrow V = \frac{Mvsin\theta}{m+M} = \frac{Msin\theta}{m+M}\sqrt{\frac{2gL(m+M)sin\theta}{m+Mcos^2\theta}}; \ [From \ eq(vii)]$$

$$\rightarrow V = \sqrt{\frac{2gLM^2(m+M)sin^3\theta}{(m+M)^2(m+Mcos^2\theta)}} \qquad ANS$$

EXAMPLE: In the below figure, a big disc of mass M and radius R, is placed over frictionless horizontal plane. Another small disc of mass m and radius r is moving with velocity u over frictionless horizontal plane as shown, strikes with the bigger disc elastically.

(*i*) Find out the final velocities of COM of both discs in ground frame.

(*ii*) Find out the linear impulse imparted to the big disc by the small disc.

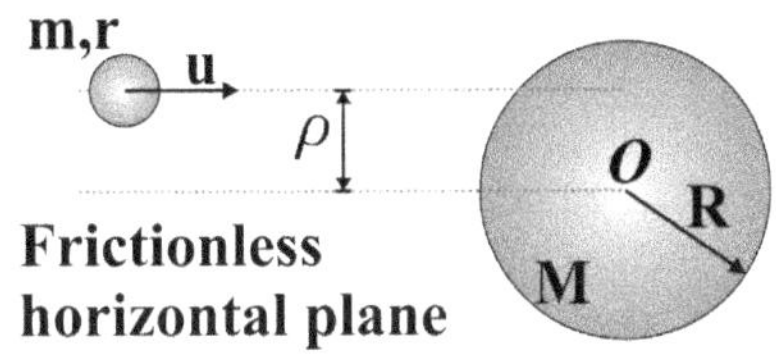

SOLUTION: (*i*) See the next fig (a) and (b) for the reference. Just before impact, the actual vel of the small disc was u and that of big disc was zero. Suppose that the straight line *OO'* is *x*-axis as shown.

As we can simply realise that the impulsive action and reaction forces shall act along the *x*-axis during the impact, hence it will be defined as the 'line of impact'. We have already learnt that the linear momentum/velocity component of both will change along the line of impact but it will not change along the *y*-axis, because there is no force acting on

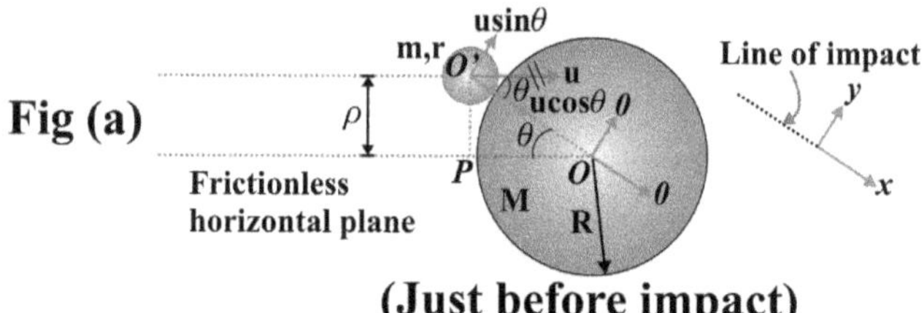

Fig (a)

(Just before impact)

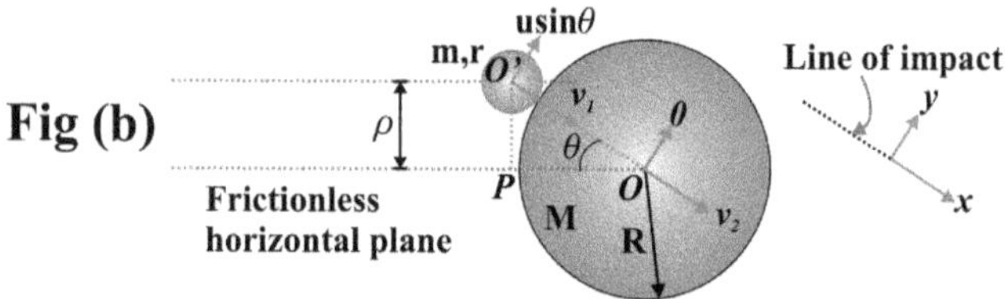

Fig (b)

(Just after impact)

each along the y-axis. Hence, just after impact the x-component and y-component of the velocity of the small disc will be v_1 and $u\sin\theta$ respectively. Just after impact the x-component and y-component of the velocity of the big disc will be v_2 and zero respectively. Applying momentum conservation along x-axis:

$mu\cos\theta + 0 = mv_1 + Mv_2 \rightarrow mu\cos\theta = mv_1 + Mv_2 - (i)$

Applying the Newton's equation along x-axis:

|vel of recession| = e|vel of approach|

$\rightarrow v_2 - v_1 = (1)(u\cos\theta - 0) \rightarrow v_2 - v_1 = u\cos\theta - (ii)$ [elastic impact: e=1]

From the triangle OPO':

$$\sin\theta = \frac{\rho}{R+r}, \cos\theta = \frac{\sqrt{(R+r)^2 - \rho^2}}{R+r}$$

From eq (i) and (ii): $v_2 = v_1 + u\cos\theta$

but $mu\cos\theta = mv_1 + Mv_2 \rightarrow mu\cos\theta = mv_1 + M(v_1 + u\cos\theta)$

$\rightarrow mu\cos\theta = (m+M)v_1 + Mu\cos\theta \rightarrow v_1 = \dfrac{(m-M)u\cos\theta}{(m+M)}$

Since $v_2 = v_1 + u\cos\theta = \dfrac{(m-M)u\cos\theta}{(m+M)} + u\cos\theta$

$$\rightarrow v_2 = \left(\frac{(m-M)}{(m+M)} + 1 \right) u \cos\theta = \frac{2mu\cos\theta}{(m+M)}$$

Now, just after impact :

$$\text{Actual vel of m} = \sqrt{v_1^2 + (u\sin\theta)^2}$$

$$\text{Actual vel of m} = u\sqrt{\left(\frac{(m-M)\cos\theta}{(m+M)} \right)^2 + (\sin\theta)^2} \quad \text{ANS}$$

$$\text{Actual vel of M} = v_2 = \frac{2mu\cos\theta}{(m+M)} \quad \text{ANS}$$

(*ii*) The linear impulse imparted to the big disc by the

small disc $= \vec{I}_l =$ Change in momentum of the big disc

$$\rightarrow \vec{I}_l = \Delta\vec{p}_M = \vec{p}_f - \vec{p}_i = M\vec{v}_2 - \vec{0} = Mv_2\hat{i}$$

$$\rightarrow \vec{I}_l = M\left(\frac{2mu\cos\theta}{(m+M)} \right)\hat{i} = \left(\frac{2mMu\cos\theta}{(m+M)} \right)\hat{i} \quad \text{ANS}$$

EXAMPLE: In the next figure, there is a frictionless rigid horizontal plane. A frictionless small semi elastic ball of mass m strikes the plane with a striking velocity u, at a striking angle of 30^0. Then, find out:
(*i*)the rebounding velocity,
(*ii*)the linear impulse $\vec{I}_l$ imparted to the ball by the rigid plane,

(*iii*)the average impulsive reaction force $< \vec{N} >$ applied by the rigid plane on the small ball, if the collision period is Δt.

NOTE:
The collision is very strong. The coefficient of restitution e=1/2.

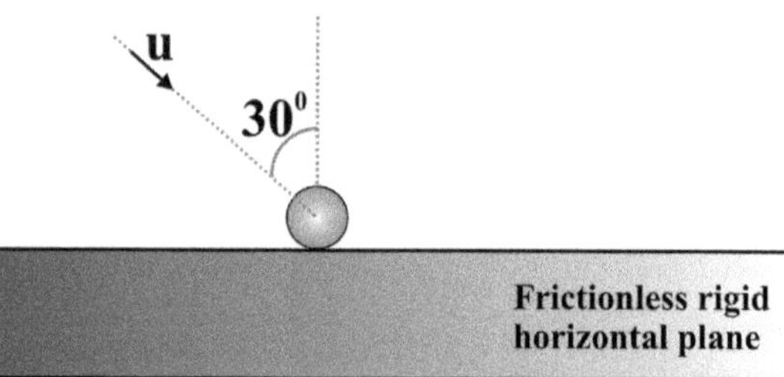

SOLUTION: See the above figure for just before impact. Since the collision is very strong, hence the gravity force on the ball can be ignored as compared to the average impulsive reaction force $<\vec{N}>$ on the ball. We have already learnt that the $<\vec{N}>\uparrow\uparrow \vec{I}_l$, as shown in the figure.

Consider x and y components of the striking velocity u as u_x=usin30 and u_y=-ucos30. In vector notations:

$$\vec{u} = u\sin 30\hat{i} - u\cos 30\hat{j} = (u/2)(\hat{i} - \sqrt{3}\hat{j})$$

Suppose just after impact, x and y components of the rebounding velocity v are v_x and v_y as shown in the next figure. Since there is no force along x-axis hence v_x=u_x.

That is: v_x=usin30=u/2. Along y-axis (line of impact), applying Newton's equation. That is:

|vel of recession|=e|vel of approach|

$\rightarrow |v_y|=(1/2)|u_y| \rightarrow |v_y|=(1/2)(\sqrt{3}/2)u \rightarrow v_y=+(\sqrt{3}/4)u$

(*i*) Therefore, the rebounding velocity:

$$\vec{v} = v_x\hat{i} + v_y\hat{j} = (u/2)\hat{i} + (u\sqrt{3}/4)\hat{j} = (u/4)(2\hat{i} + \sqrt{3}\hat{j}) \quad \text{ANS}$$

(*ii*) The linear impulse $\vec{I}_l$ imparted to the ball by the rigid plane:

$$\vec{I}_l = \Delta\vec{p}_{ball} = \text{Change in the linear momentum of the ball}$$

$$\rightarrow \vec{I}_l = m\vec{v} - m\vec{u} = m(\vec{v} - \vec{u}) = m[(u/4)(2\hat{i} + \sqrt{3}\hat{j}) - (u/2)(\hat{i} - \sqrt{3}\hat{j})]$$

$$\rightarrow \vec{I}_l = (mu/4)(3\sqrt{3}\hat{j}) = [3\sqrt{3}/4]mu\hat{j} \quad \text{ANS}$$

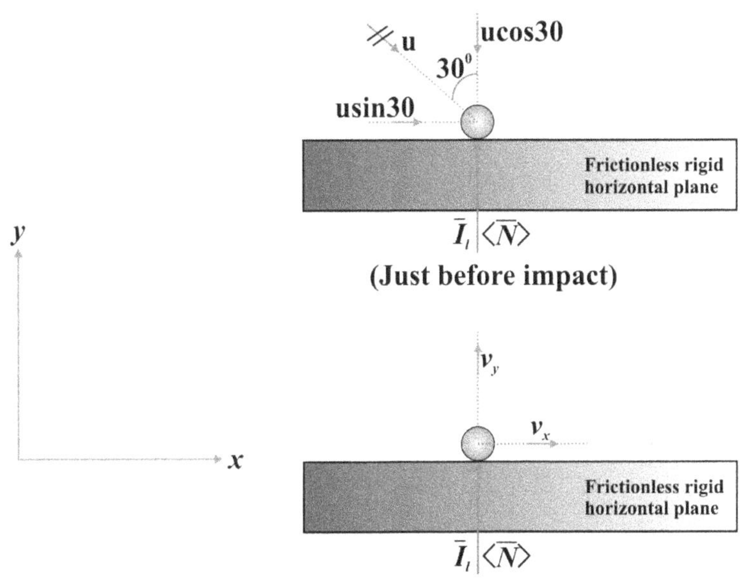

(Just after impact)

(*iii*) The average impulsive reaction force $< \vec{N} >$ applied by the rigid plane on the small ball, if the collision period is Δt:

We have already learned that : $\vec{I_I} =< \vec{N} > \Delta t = \Delta \vec{p}_{body}$

$$\rightarrow < \vec{N} >= \frac{\Delta \vec{p}_{body}}{\Delta t} = \frac{\vec{I_I}}{\Delta t} = \frac{3\sqrt{3}}{4} \frac{mu}{\Delta t} \hat{j} \quad \text{ANS}$$

EXAMPLE: Three point-masses of 2g, 3g and 4g are placed at the vertices of an equilateral triangle of side 1 meter. Find the distance of the centre of mass of the system from the point-mass 2g.

SOLUTION: See the next figure for the reference. Suppose m_1=2g, m_2=3g, m_3=4g and L=1m. Place m_1=2g at the origin O intentionally. Suppose the coordinates of m_1, m_2 & m_3 are (x_1, y_1), (x_2, y_2) & (x_3, y_3) respectively.

Now, we can easily calculate that: $x_1=0$, $y_1=0$; $x_2=1$m, $y_2=0$ and $x_3=Lcos60=1/2$m, $y_3=Lsin60=\sqrt{3}/2$m.

We already know that the coordinates of the COM of three particle system are given as:

$$x_{CM} = \frac{\Sigma(m_i x_i)}{\Sigma(m_i)} = \frac{m_1 x_1 + m_2 x_2 + m_3 x_3}{m_1 + m_2 + m_3}$$

$$y_{CM} = \frac{\Sigma(m_i y_i)}{\Sigma(m_i)} = \frac{m_1 y_1 + m_2 y_2 + m_3 y_3}{m_1 + m_2 + m_3}$$

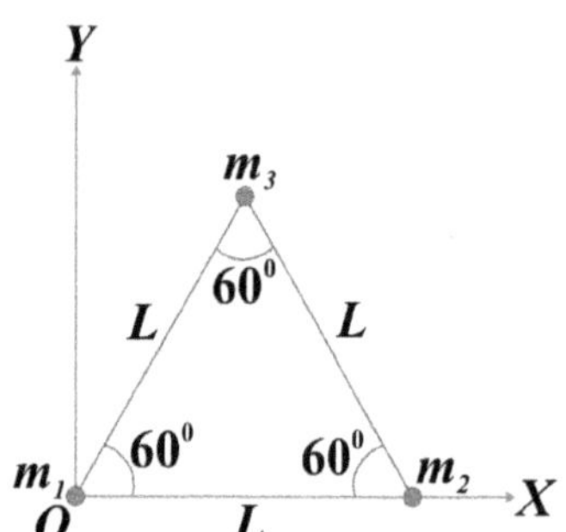

$$\rightarrow y_{CM} = \frac{(2)(0) + (3)(0) + (4)(\sqrt{3}/2)}{(2) + (3) + (4)} = \frac{2\sqrt{3}}{9}\,\text{m}$$

The distance between the origin $O(0,0)$ & COM (x_{CM}, y_{CM}):

$$OC = \sqrt{x_{CM}^2 + y_{CM}^2} = \sqrt{\left(\frac{5}{9}\right)^2 + \left(\frac{2\sqrt{3}}{9}\right)^2} = \frac{1}{9}\sqrt{25 + 12} = \frac{\sqrt{37}}{9}\,\text{m,}$$

ANS

EXAMPLE: Three particles of masses 100 g, 150 g and 200 g are placed at the vertices of an equilateral triangle. Each side of the triangle is 0.5 m long. Locate COM of the system with respect to 100 g.

SOLUTION: See the next figure for the reference. Suppose m_1=100 g, m_2=150 g, m_3=200 g and L=0.5 m. Place m_1=100 g at the origin O intentionally.

Suppose the coordinates of m_1, m_2 & m_3 are (x_1, y_1), (x_2, y_2) & (x_3, y_3) respectively. Now, we can easily calculate that:

x_1=0, y_1=0; x_2=0.5 m, y_2=0, and

x_3=$L\cos60$ =(0.5)(1/2)=0.25 m,

y_3=$L\sin60$=(0.5)($\sqrt{3}/2$) =0.43 m.

We already know that the coordinates of the COM of three particle system are given as:

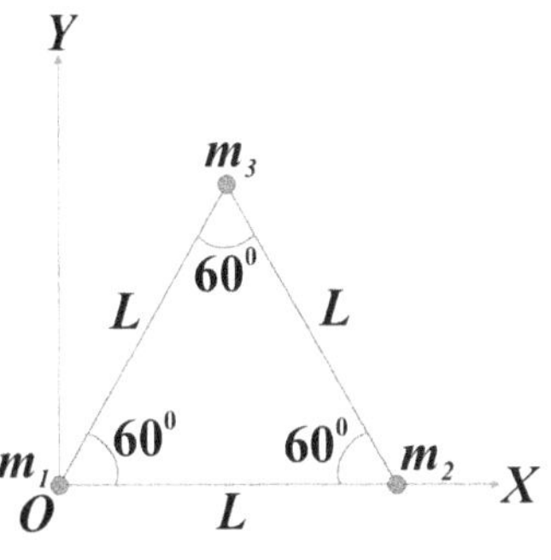

$$x_{CM} = \frac{\Sigma(m_i x_i)}{\Sigma(m_i)} = \frac{m_1 x_1 + m_2 x_2 + m_3 x_3}{m_1 + m_2 + m_3}$$

$$y_{CM} = \frac{\Sigma(m_i y_i)}{\Sigma(m_i)} = \frac{m_1 y_1 + m_2 y_2 + m_3 y_3}{m_1 + m_2 + m_3}$$

$$\rightarrow x_{CM} = \frac{(100)(0) + (150)(0.5) + (200)(0.25)}{(100) + (150) + (200)} = 0.28\text{m}$$

$$\rightarrow y_{CM} = \frac{(100)(0) + (150)(0) + (200)(0.43)}{(100) + (150) + (200)} = 0.19\text{m}$$

The distance between the origin $O(0,0)$ & COM (x_{CM}, y_{CM}):

$$OC = \sqrt{x_{CM}^2 + y_{CM}^2} = \sqrt{(0.28)^2 + (0.19)^2} = \sqrt{0.078 + 0.036}$$

$OC = 0.34\text{m} \qquad$ ANS

EXAMPLE: Three identical homogeneous spheres A, B and C, each of radius R, are placed touching one another on a horizontal table. What is the distance of centre of mass of the system from the centre of A?

SOLUTION: See the next figure for the reference. Since all the three spheres are identical and homogeneous, hence their COM will be located at the geometrical centre of the system, that is at point O. This is very clear from the diagram that:

In the right angled triangle OPA : $\cos 30 = \dfrac{AP}{AO} \rightarrow \dfrac{\sqrt{3}}{2} = \dfrac{R}{AO}$

$\rightarrow AO = 2R/\sqrt{3} \qquad$ ANS

EXAMPLE: A shell of mass 200 gm is ejected from a gun of mass 4 kg by an explosion that generates 1.05 kJ of energy. The initial velocity of the shell is:

(a) 80 ms^{-1}

(b) 40 ms^{-1}

(c) 120 ms^{-1}

(d) 100 ms^{-1}

SOLUTION: If we ignore all external forces acting on the gun-shell system, as compared to the internal impulsive separating forces, then the linear momentum of the system will remain conserved. That is: $p_{just\ before\ explosion} = p_{just\ after\ explosion}$.

But since $p_{just\ before\ explosion} = 0$, hence $p_{just\ after\ explosion} = 0$.

This will happen only if both bodies move in the opposite direction. That is: $+m_{shell}\ v_{shell} - m_{gun}\ v_{gun} = 0$

$\rightarrow |p_{shell}| = |p_{gun}| = x$ (say)

Given that: $K_{total} = 1.05$ kJ $= 1050$ J $\rightarrow K_{shell} + K_{gun} = 1050$ J

$$\rightarrow \frac{|p_{shell}|^2}{2m_{shell}} + \frac{|p_{gun}|^2}{2m_{gun}} = 1050 \text{ J} \rightarrow \frac{x^2}{2(0.2)} + \frac{x^2}{2(4)} = 1050 \text{ J}$$

$$\rightarrow x^2(5 + 0.25) = 2100 \text{ J} \rightarrow x^2 = \frac{2100}{5.25} = 400 \rightarrow x = 20 \text{ kgms}^{-1}$$

$$\rightarrow x = p_{shell} = m_{shell} v_{shell} \rightarrow v_{shell} = \frac{x}{m_{shell}} = \frac{20}{0.2} = 100 \text{ ms}^{-1}$$

$$\rightarrow v_{shell} = 100 \text{ ms}^{-1} \rightarrow \text{OPTION (d)}$$

EXAMPLE: An explosion blows a rock into three parts in free space. Two parts go off at right angles to each other. These two are 1 kg first part moving with a velocity of 12 m/s & 2 kg second part moving with a velocity 8 m/s. If the third part flies off with a velocity of 4 m/s, its momentum would be:

(a) 20 kgm/s

(b) 7 kgm/s

(c) 17 kgm/s

(d) 3 kgm/s

SOLUTION: Suppose the external forces acting on the rock are negligible as compared to the internal impulsive separating forces. Hence, the linear momentum vector of the whole system will remain conserved. That is:

$$\vec{P}_{\text{just before explosion}} = \vec{P}_{\text{just afterexplosion}}$$

But since $\vec{p}_{\text{just before explosion}} = 0$, hence $\vec{p}_{\text{just after explosion}} = \vec{0}$

$$\to \vec{p}_1 + \vec{p}_2 + \vec{p}_3 = \vec{0} \to \vec{p}_3 = -(\vec{p}_1 + \vec{p}_2) \to \left|\vec{p}_3\right| = \left|\vec{p}_1 + \vec{p}_2\right|$$

$$\to \left|\vec{p}_3\right| = \sqrt{\left|\vec{p}_1\right|^2 + \left|\vec{p}_2\right|^2}, \text{ because } \vec{p}_1 \text{ \& } \vec{p}_2 \text{ are perpendicular.}$$

$$\to \left|\vec{p}_3\right| = \sqrt{\left|m_1 v_1\right|^2 + \left|m_2 v_2\right|^2} = \sqrt{\left|(1\text{kg})(12\text{ms}^{-1})\right|^2 + \left|(2\text{kg})(8\text{ms}^{-1})\right|^2}$$

$$\to \left|\vec{p}_3\right| = \sqrt{144 + 256} = \sqrt{400} = 20 \text{ kgms}^{-1} \quad \to \text{OPTION (a)}$$

EXAMPLE: Two identical particles move towards each other with velocity $2v$ and v respectively. The speed of center of mass is:

(a) v

(b) $v/3$

(c) $v/2$

(d) zero

SOLUTION: Since the vectors are one-dimensional, we should make a sign convention. Suppose the rightward vector is +ve and the leftward vector is -ve.

Then $v_1 = +2v$, $v_2 = -v$, $m_1 = m_2 = m$. We know that the velocity of COM of two particle systems is:

$$v_C = \frac{m_1 v_1 + m_2 v_2}{m_1 + m_2} = \frac{m(+2v) + m(-v)}{m + m} = \frac{v}{2} \to \text{OPTION (c)}$$

EXAMPLE: A body A of mass M while falling vertically downwards under gravity breaks into two parts, a body B of mass $2M/3$ and a body C of mass $M/3$. Ignore air resistance. The centre of mass of bodies B and C taken together shifts compared to that of body A towards:

(a) depends on height of breaking.

(b) does not shift.

(c) body C.

(d) body B.

SOLUTION: Since just before explosion, just after explosion and during the explosion, the only external force acting on $(B+C)$ system is gravity force; vertically downwards hence according to the Newton's second law the COM of $(B+C)$ system will continuously move with constant acceleration $\vec{g}$ in the downward vertical direction. Therefore, it will not shift in the horizontal direction. $\rightarrow$ OPTION (b)

EXAMPLE: The block of mass M moving on the frictionless horizontal surface collides with the spring of spring constant k and compresses it by length L. The maximum momentum of the block after collision is:

(a) $\sqrt{Mk}\ L$

(b) $kL^2 / 2M$

(c) zero

(d) ML^2 / k

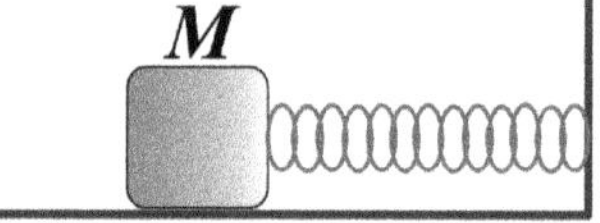

SOLUTION: Suppose at the moment when the block of mass M just touches the spring, the speed of the block is v. As the block compresses the spring its speed will decrease hence its linear momentum will also decrease. After some time, it will bounce back and the block will again acquire its original speed v and hence maximum momentum, when the spring is totally relaxed. During this process, the total mechanical energy of (block+spring) system will remain conserved. That is, during the relaxation process, the loss in elastic potential energy of the spring=gain in the kinetic energy of the block M.

$$\to \frac{1}{2}kL^2 - 0 = \frac{1}{2}Mv^2 - 0 \to \frac{1}{2}kL^2 = \frac{1}{2}\frac{p_{max}^2}{M} \to p_{max}^2 = MkL^2$$

$$\to p_{max} = \sqrt{Mk}L \qquad \to \text{OPTION (a)}$$

EXAMPLE: A mass m moves with a velocity v and collides with another identical mass at rest. After collision the 1st mass moves with velocity $v/\sqrt{3}$ in a direction perpendicular to the initial direction of motion. Find the speed of the 2nd mass after collision:

(a) v

(b) $\sqrt{3}v$

(c) $2v/\sqrt{3}$

(d) $v/\sqrt{3}$

SOLUTION: If we ignore all external forces acting on $(A+B)$ system, then the linear momentum vector will remain conserved. Suppose the particle B acquires velocity $(v_x \hat{i} + v_y \hat{j})$ just after impact as shown.

(Just before impact)

(Just after impact)

Applying momentum conservation along the x-axis:

$mv+0=0+mv_x \to v_x=v$ -(i)

Applying momentum conservation along the y-axis:

$0+0=+mv_y-m[v/\sqrt{3}] \to v_y=v/\sqrt{3}$ -(ii)

So, the speed of the 2nd mass after collision:

$$v_{Bf} = \sqrt{v_x^2 + v_y^2} = \sqrt{(v)^2 + \left(\frac{v}{\sqrt{3}}\right)^2} = v\sqrt{1 + \frac{1}{3}} = \frac{2v}{\sqrt{3}} \to \text{OPTION (c)}$$

EXAMPLE: A (T) shaped object with dimensions shown in the figure, is lying on a horizontal frictionless floor. A force $\vec{F}$ is applied at the point P parallel to AB, such that the object has only the translational motion without rotation. Find the location of P with respect to C. (T) is made of similar type of rods.

(a) $2l/3$ (b) $3l/2$

(c) $4l/3$ (d) l

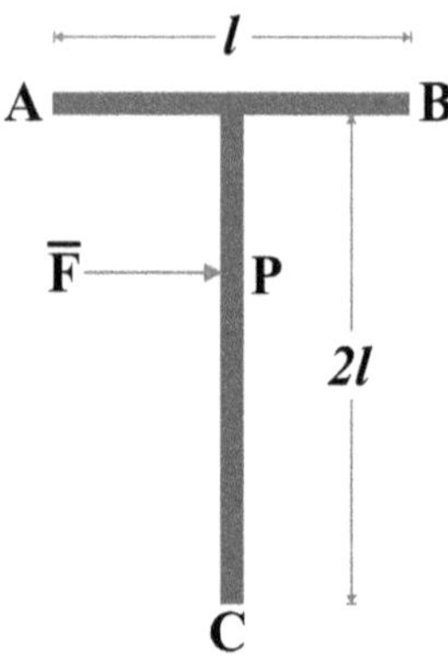

SOLUTION: When a force $\vec{F}$ is applied at the point P parallel to AB, such that the object has only the translational motion without rotation. It means the point P is itself COM of the whole system. Since (T) is made of similar type of rods, hence mass of the rod will be directly proportional to its length. So, for the vertical rod $m_1=2m$, for the horizontal rod $m_2=m$.

Suppose the centre of mass of the vertical rod is C_1, hence $y_1=l$ and the centre of mass of the horizontal rod is C_2, hence $y_2=2l$. The common COM of the (T) object must lie on the axis of symmetry, that is Y-axis.

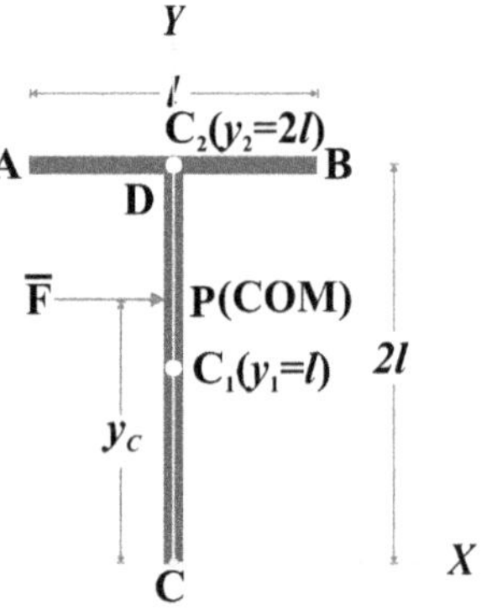

It must be point P ($y_C=y_C$). We already know that:

$$y_C = CP = \frac{m_1 y_1 + m_2 y_2}{m_1 + m_2} = \frac{2ml + m2l}{2m + m} = \frac{4ml}{3m} = \frac{4l}{3} \rightarrow \text{OPTION (c)}$$

EXAMPLE: A bomb of mass 16 kg at rest explodes into two pieces of masses 4 kg and 12 kg. The velocity of the 12 kg mass is 4m/s. The kinetic energy of the other mass is:

(a) 192 J   (b) 96 J

(c) 144 J   (d) 288 J

SOLUTION: Since the bomb of mass 16 kg at rest explodes into two pieces of masses 4 kg and 12 kg, hence its initial momentum will be zero. If we ignore all other external forces as compared to internal separating forces, acting on (4 kg+12 kg) system then the linear momentum of COM of the given system will remain conserved. That is, just after explosion the final momentum of the system will also remain zero. Given that: M=16 kg, v=0, m_1=4 kg, m_2=12 kg, v_1=?, v_2=-4 m/s.

Initial momentum=0→Mv=0→(16)(0)=0

Final momentum=0→$m_1v_1+m_2v_2$=0→(4)v_1+(12)(-4)=0

$$\rightarrow v_1 = 12 \text{ m / s} \rightarrow K_1 = \frac{1}{2}m_1v_1^2 = \frac{1}{2}(4)(12)^2 = (2)(144) = 288 \text{ J}$$

$\rightarrow$ OPTION (d)

NOTE: Since there are only two masses after explosion, they are bound to move along the same straight line in opposite direction to make their resultant momentum zero.

EXAMPLE: A player caught a cricket ball of mass 150 g moving at a rate of 20 m/s. If the catching process is completed in 0.1 s, the force of the blow exerted by the ball on the hands of the player is equal to:

(a)30 N   (b)300 N

(c)150 N   (d)3 N

SOLUTION: See the adjacent fig for reference. We can simply ignore the gravity force on the ball as compared to the force of blow N on the ball by the hands. According to the Newton's second law:

$$N = \frac{dp}{dt} \rightarrow N = \frac{p_2 - p_1}{t_2 - t_1} = \frac{mv_2 - (-mu)}{t - 0}$$

$$\rightarrow N = \frac{m(v_2 + u)}{t} = \frac{(0.15kg)(0+20)m/s}{0.1s} \rightarrow N = (1.5)(20) = 30 \text{ newton}$$

According to the Newton's third law:

The force of blow on the ball by the hands=The force of blow on the hands by the ball=30 newton   →OPTION (a)

EXAMPLE: Consider a two-particle system with particles having masses m_1 and m_2. If the first particle is pushed towards the centre of mass through a distance d, by what distance should the second particle be moved, so as to keep the centre of mass at the same position?

(a) $\dfrac{m_1}{m_2} d$

(b) d

(c) $\dfrac{m_2}{m_1} d$

(d) $\dfrac{m_1}{m_1+m_2} d$

SOLUTION: Since we have to keep the COM at the same position, hence $\Delta x_C = 0$. Given: $\Delta x_1 = +d$, $|\Delta x_2| = ?$

We have already learned that : $x_C = \dfrac{m_1 x_1 + m_2 x_2}{m_1 + m_2}$

$$\to \Delta x_C = \frac{m_1 \Delta x_1 + m_2 \Delta x_2}{m_1 + m_2} \to 0 = \frac{m_1(+d) + m_2 \Delta x_2}{m_1 + m_2}$$

$$\to m_1 d + m_2 \Delta x_2 = 0 \to \Delta x_2 = -\frac{m_1}{m_2} d \to |\Delta x_2| = \frac{m_1}{m_2} d$$

→ OPTION (a)

EXAMPLE: A circular disc of radius R is removed from a bigger circular disc of radius 2R such that the circumference of the discs coincide. The centre of mass of the new disc is αR from the centre of the bigger disc. The value of α is: [$|\alpha| > 0$]

(a) 1/6

(b) 1/4

(c) 1/3

(d) 1/2

SOLUTION: Suppose the uniform mass density of the solid portion of the given disc is σ kg/m^2. Now, consider uncut body, cut portion and the remaining body as shown below. We can simply realise that the mass distribution is symmetrical about the shown x-axis. Hence, the position of COM in each case will be situated on the x-axis itself as shown in the next figure.

For the uncut body, $x_{uncut}=0$.

For the cut portion, $x_{cut}=+R$.

For the remaining body, suppose it is given: $x_{res}=x_c$ (unknown)

$$x_{res}=x_c=\frac{m_{uncut}\,x_{uncut}-m_{cut}\,x_{cut}}{m_{uncut}-m_{cut}}=\frac{\sigma\pi(2R)^2(0)-\sigma\pi(R)^2(+R)}{\sigma\pi(2R)^2-\sigma\pi(R)^2}$$

Uncut body   **Remaining body**

Cut portion

$$\to x_c=-\frac{R}{3}\to|x_c|=\frac{R}{3}\to\alpha R=\frac{R}{3}\to\alpha=\frac{1}{3}\to\text{OPTION (c)}$$

XAMPLE: A thin rod of length L is lying along the x-axis with its ends at $x = 0$ and $x = L$. Its linear mass density (mass/length) varies with x as $k\left(x/L\right)^{n}$, where n can be zero or any positive number. If the position x_{CM} of the centre of mass of the rod is plotted against 'n', which of the following graphs best approximates the dependence of x_{CM} on n?

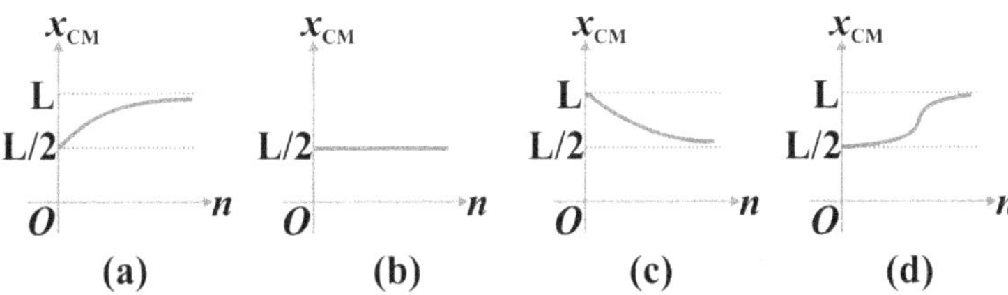

SOLUTION: See the next figure for the reference. Given that

$$\lambda = k(x/L)^n$$

the linear mass density of a stick is: $\lambda = k\left(x/L\right)^n$, where $n \geq 0$.

We already know that for a continuum system, the x-coordinate of its COM:

$$x_c = \frac{\int\limits_{x=0}^{x=L} dm\,x}{\int\limits_{x=0}^{x=L} dm}, \text{ but given that } \frac{dm}{dx} = k\left(x/L\right)^n \rightarrow dm = k\left(x/L\right)^n dx$$

$$x_c = \frac{\int\limits_{x=0}^{x=L} k\left(x/L\right)^n x\,dx}{\int\limits_{x=0}^{x=L} k\left(x/L\right)^n dx} = \frac{\int\limits_{x=0}^{x=L} \left(x^{n+1}\right)dx}{\int\limits_{x=0}^{x=L} \left(x^n\right)dx} = \frac{\left.\dfrac{x^{n+2}}{n+2}\right|_0^L}{\left.\dfrac{x^{n+1}}{n+1}\right|_0^L} = \left.\frac{n+1}{n+2}x\right|_0^L = \frac{n+1}{n+2}L$$

$$x_c = \frac{n+1}{n+2}L. \text{ As } n = 0, x_c = \frac{L}{2}$$

$$\text{As } n \rightarrow \infty, x_c = \frac{1+\dfrac{1}{n}}{1+\dfrac{2}{n}}L = \frac{1+\dfrac{1}{\infty}}{1+\dfrac{2}{\infty}}L = L \rightarrow \left(\begin{array}{l}\text{It means as } n \text{ varies}\\ \text{from 0 to } \infty \text{ ,} x_c \text{varies}\\ \text{from } (L/2) \text{ to } L.\end{array}\right)$$

Hence, correct answer is OPTION(a).

Because slope of the curve$= \dfrac{dx}{dn} = \dfrac{1}{(n+2)^2}L > 0$ at $n=0$

and slope of the curve$= \dfrac{dx}{dn} = 0$ at $n=\infty$.

EXAMPLE: A body of mass m = 3.513 kg is moving along the x-axis with a speed of 5.00 ms^{-1}. The magnitude of its momentum is recorded as:

(a)17.6 kg m/s   (b)17.565 kg m/s

(c)17.56 kg m/s   (d)17.57 kg m/s

SOLUTION: The magnitude of momentum recorded:

$p=mv=(3.513 \text{ kg})(5.00 \text{ ms}^{-1})=\underline{17.565} \text{ kg m/s}$

In the quantity mass m, there are 4 significant figures. In the quantity velocity v, there are 3 significant figures. Hence, the final quantity momentum p will be rounded off upto least number of significant figures, that is 3. The rounded off value of momentum p=17.6 kg m/s $\rightarrow$OPTION (a)

EXAMPLE: Consider a rubber ball freely falling from a height $h = 4.9\ m$ onto a horizontal elastic plate. Assume that the duration of collision is negligible and the collision with the plate is totally elastic. Then the velocity as a function of time and the height as a function of time will be:

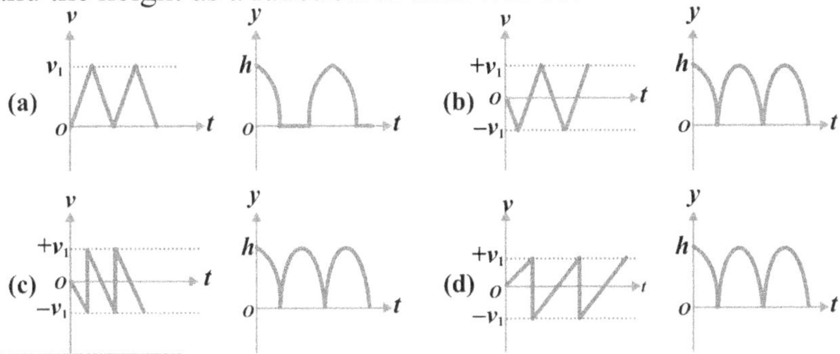

SOLUTION: When a rubber ball freely falling from a height $h = 4.9\ m$ onto a horizontal elastic plate, then it is clear that before the first collision with the plate, the direction of velocity vector v will be downwards hence conventionally its sign should be negative but its magnitude would be increasing with time t. However, height vector y will be upwards; its sign will be positive but the magnitude would be decreasing with time t. Just after the first impact, its velocity vector v suddenly changes from $-v_1$ to $+v_1$ within no time.

All these conditions are simultaneously satisfied in option (c), hence the correct answer is OPTION (c).

TRYOUT SUPPLEMENT

All problems have been divided into two parts:

(i)Galaxy: JEE (main)/SAT Subject Test archive [advanced]

(ii)Universal: IIT-JEE (advanced)/KVPY/NTSE/Olympiads archive [advanced]

Galaxy: JEE (main)/SAT Subject Test ARCHIVE

P01. A circular plate of diameter d is kept in contact with a square plate of edge d as shown in figure. The density of the material and the thickness are same everywhere. The center of mass of the composite system will be:

(a) inside the circular plate.

(b) inside the square plate.

(c) at the point of contact.

(d) outside the system.

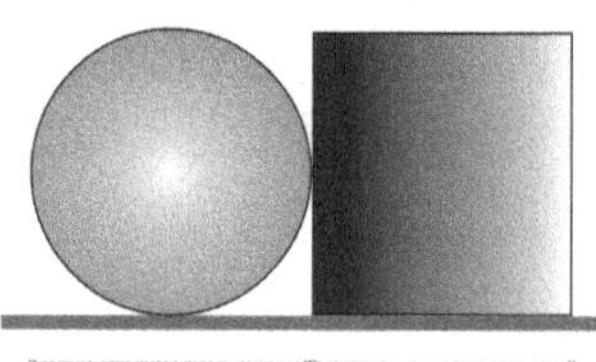

P02. Consider a system of two identical particles. One of the particles is at rest and the other has an acceleration $\vec{a}$. The center of mass has an acceleration:

(a) zero

(b) $(1/2)\vec{a}$

(c) $\vec{a}$

(d) $2\vec{a}$

P03. A uniform sphere is placed on a smooth horizontal surface and a horizontal force F is applied on it at a distance h above the surface. The acceleration of the center of mass:

(a) is maximum when $h= 0$.

(b) is maximum when $h=R$.

(c) is maximum when $h=2R$.

(d) is independent of h.

P04. A ball kept in a closed box moves in the box making collisions with the walls. The box is kept on a smooth horizontal surface. The velocity of the center of mass:

(a)of the box remains constant.

(b)of the 'box plus the ball' system remains constant.

(c)of the ball remains constant.

(d)of the ball relative to the box remains constant.

P05. A body at rest breaks in free space, into two pieces of equal masses. The parts will move:
(a) in same direction.
(b) along different lines.
(c) in opposite directions with equal speeds.
(d) in opposite directions with unequal speeds.

P06. The quantities remaining constant in an elastic collision are:
(a) momentum, kinetic energy and temperature.
(b) momentum and kinetic energy but not temperature.
(c) momentum and temperature but not kinetic energy.
(d) momentum, but neither kinetic energy nor temperature.

P07. A nucleus moving with a velocity $\vec{v}$ emits an α-particle. Let the velocities of the α-particle and the remaining nucleus be $\vec{v}_1$ and $\vec{v}_2$ and their masses be m_1 and m_2.
(a) $\vec{v}$, $\vec{v}_1$ and $\vec{v}_2$ must be parallel to each other.
(b) None of the two of $\vec{v}, \vec{v}_1$ and $\vec{v}_2$ should be parallel to each other.
(c) $\vec{v}_1 + \vec{v}_2$ must be parallel to $\vec{v}$.
(d) $m_1\vec{v}_1 + m_2\vec{v}_2$ must be parallel to $\vec{v}$.

P08. The position vector of centre of mass of a system of particles directly depends upon:
(a) masses of particles.
(b) forces acting on the particles.
(c) position vectors of the particles.
(d) momentum of the particles.

P09. In carbon monoxide molecules, the carbon and the oxygen atoms are separated by a distance 1.12×10^{-10} m. The distance of the centre of mass, from the carbon atom is:
(a) 0.64×10^{-10} m (b) 0.56×10^{-10} m
(c) 0.51×10^{-10} m (d) 0.48×10^{-10} m

P10. Two spheres of masses 2M and M are initially at rest at a distance R apart in free space. Due to mutual force of attraction, they approach each other. When they are at separation R/2, the acceleration of the centre of mass of spheres would be:

(a) 0 m/s^2 (b) g m/s^2

(c) 3 g m/s^2 (d) 12 g m/s^2

P11. A shell of mass 200 gm is ejected from a gun of mass 4 kg by an explosion that generates 1.05 kJ of energy. The initial velocity of the shell is:

(a) 80 ms^{-1} (b) 40 ms^{-1}

(c) 120 ms^{-1} (d) 100 ms^{-1}

P12. An explosion blows a rock into three parts in free space. Two parts go off at right angles to each other. These two are 1 kg first part moving with a velocity of 12 m/s & 2 kg second part moving with a velocity 8 m/s. If the third part flies off with a velocity of 4 m/s, its momentum would be:

(a) 20 kgm/s   (b) 7 kgm/s

(c) 17 kgm/s   (d) 3 kgm/s

P13. A body A of mass M while falling vertically downwards under gravity breaks into two parts, a body B of mass $2M/3$ and, a body C of mass $M/3$. The centre of mass of bodies B and C taken together shifts compared to that of body A towards:

(a) depends on height of breaking.

(b) does not shift.

(c) body C.

(d) body B.

P14. A mass m moves with a velocity v and collides inelastically with another identical mass at rest. After collision the 1st mass moves with velocity $v/\sqrt{3}$ in a direction perpendicular to the initial direction of motion. Find the speed of the 2nd mass after collision:

(a) v (b) $\sqrt{3}v$

(c) $2v/\sqrt{3}$ (d) $v/\sqrt{3}$

P15. A bomb of mass 16 kg at rest explodes into two pieces of masses 4 kg and 12 kg. The velocity of the 12 kg mass is 4m/s. The kinetic energy of the other mass is:

(a)192 J (b)96 J

(c)144 J (d)288 J

P16. Consider a two-particle system with particles having masses m_1 and m_2. If the first particle is pushed towards the centre of mass through a distance d, by what distance should the second particle be moved, so as to keep the centre of mass at the same position?

(a) $\dfrac{m_1}{m_2} d$ (b)d

(c) $\dfrac{m_2}{m_1} d$ (d) $\dfrac{m_1}{m_1 + m_2} d$

P17. A circular disc of radius R is removed from a bigger circular disc of radius $2R$ such that the circumference of the discs coincide. The centre of mass of the new disc is αR from the centre of the bigger disc. The value of α is:

(a)1/6 (b)1/4

(c)1/3 (d)1/2

P18. A body of mass m = 3.513 kg is moving along the x-axis with a speed of 5.00 ms^{-1}. The magnitude of its momentum is recorded as:

(a)17.6 kg m/s

(b)17.565 kg m/s

(c)17.56 kg m/s

(d)17.57 kg m/s

P19. A mass m moving horizontally (along the x-axis) with velocity v collides and sticks to a mass of $3m$ moving vertically upward (along the y-axis) with velocity $2v$. The final velocity of the combination is: [Ignore all external forces acting on the two-mass system.]

(a) $\dfrac{1}{3}v\hat{i}+\dfrac{2}{3}v\hat{j}$

(b) $\dfrac{2}{3}v\hat{i}+\dfrac{1}{3}v\hat{j}$

(c) $\dfrac{3}{2}v\hat{i}+\dfrac{1}{4}v\hat{j}$

(d) $\dfrac{1}{4}v\hat{i}+\dfrac{3}{2}v\hat{j}$

P20. A body of mass M normally hits a rigid wall with velocity V and bounces back with the same velocity. The impulse experienced by the body is:

(a) MV

(b) 1.5 MV

(c) 2 MV

(d) zero

P21. Two spheres A and B of masses m_1 and m_2 respectively collide. A is at rest initially and B is moving with velocity v along x-axis. After collision, B has a velocity $v/2$ along $(-y)$ axis. The mass A moves after collision in the direction:

(a) $\theta = \tan^{-1}\left(\dfrac{1}{2}\right)$ to the x-axis.

(b) $\theta = \tan^{-1}\left(-\dfrac{1}{2}\right)$ to the x-axis.

(c) same as that of B.

(d) opposite to that of B.

P22. Two persons of masses 55 kg and 65 kg respectively, are at the opposite ends of a boat. The length of the boat is 3.0 m and weighs 100 kg. The 55 kg man walks up to the 65 kg man and sits with him. Ignore water friction. If the boat is in still water the center of mass of the system shifts by:

(a) zero

(b) 0.75 m

(c) 3.0 m

(d) 2.3 m

P23. This question has **Statement-I** and **Statement-II**. Of the four choices given after the statements, choose the one that best describes the two statements.

Statement–I: A particle of mass m moving with speed v collides with stationary particle of mass M. If the maximum energy loss possible is given as $f\left(\dfrac{1}{2}mv^2\right)$ then $f = \left(\dfrac{m}{M+m}\right)$.

Statement–II: Maximum energy loss occurs when the particles get stuck together as a result of the collision.

(a) **Statement–I** is true, **Statement–II** is true, **Statement–II** is a correct explanation of **Statement–I**.

(b) **Statement–I** is true, **Statement–II** is true, **Statement–II** is not a correct explanation of **Statement–I**.

(c) **Statement–I** is true, **Statement–II** is false.

(d) **Statement–I** is false, **Statement–II** is true.

P24. An explosion breaks a rock into three parts in a horizontal plane. Two of them go off at right angles to each other. The first part of mass 1 kg moves with a speed of 12 ms^{-1} and the second part of mass 2 kg moves with 8 ms^{-1} speed. If the third part flies off with 4 ms^{-1} speed, then its mass is:

(a) 17 kg   (b) 3 kg

(c) 5 kg   (d) 7 kg

P25. A body of mass $(4m)$ is lying in $x-y$ plane at rest. It suddenly explodes into three pieces. Two pieces, each of mass (m) move perpendicular to each other with equal speeds (v). The total kinetic energy generated due to explosion is:

(a) $\dfrac{3}{2}mv^2$ (b) $2\,mv^2$

(c) $4\,mv^2$ (d) mv^2

P26. Distance of the centre of mass of a solid uniform cone from its vertex is z_0. If the radius of its base is R and its height is h then z_0 is equal to:

(a) $\dfrac{3h^2}{8R}$

(b) $\dfrac{h^2}{4R}$

(c) $\dfrac{3h}{4}$

(d) $\dfrac{5h}{8}$

P27. A particle of mass m moving in the x direction with speed $2v$ is hit by another particle of mass $2m$ moving in the y direction with speed v. If the collision is perfectly inelastic, the percentage loss in the energy during the collision is close to:

(a) 62 %

(b) 44 %

(c) 50 %

(d) 56%

P28. Two spherical bodies of mass M and $5M$ and radii R and $2R$ are released in free space with initial separation between their centres equal to $12R$. If they attract each other due to gravitational force only, then the distance covered by the smaller body before collision is:

(a) $7.5R$

(b) $1.5R$

(c) $2.5R$

(d) $4.5R$

P29. Two particles of masses m_1 and m_2 move with initial velocities u_1 and u_2. On collision, one of the particles get excited to higher level, after absorbing energy ε. If final velocities of particles be v_1 and v_2, then we must have:

(a) $\dfrac{1}{2}m_1u_1^2 + \dfrac{1}{2}m_2u_2^2 - \varepsilon = \dfrac{1}{2}m_1v_1^2 + \dfrac{1}{2}m_2v_2^2$

(b) $\dfrac{1}{2}m_1^2u_1^2 + \dfrac{1}{2}m_2^2u_2^2 + \varepsilon = \dfrac{1}{2}m_1^2v_1^2 + \dfrac{1}{2}m_2^2v_2^2$

(c) $m_1^2u_1 + m_2^2u_2 - \varepsilon = m_1^2v_1 + m_2^2v_2$

(d) $\dfrac{1}{2}m_1u_1^2 + \dfrac{1}{2}m_2u_2^2 = \dfrac{1}{2}m_1v_1^2 + \dfrac{1}{2}m_2v_2^2 - \varepsilon$

P30. A bullet of mass 10g moving horizontally with a velocity of 400 ms^{-1} strikes a wooden block of mass 2kg suspended from a light inextensible string of length 5m. As a result, the

centre of gravity of the block is found to rise a vertical distance of 10 cm. The speed of the bullet after it emerges out horizontally from the block will be:
(a) 160 ms^{-1} (b) 100 ms^{-1}
(c) 80 ms^{-1} (d) 120 ms^{-1}

P31. Two identical balls A and B having velocities of 0.5 m/s and -0.3 m/s respectively collide elastically in one dimension. The velocities of B and A after the collision respectively, will be:
(a) 0.3 m/s and 0.5 m/s (b) -0.5 m/s and 0.3 m/s
(c) 0.5 m/s and -0.3 m/s (d) -0.3 m/s and 0.5 m/s

P32. Which of the following statements are correct?
(A) Center of mass of a body always coincides with the centre of gravity of the body.
(B) Centre of mass of a body is the point at which the total gravitational torque on the body is zero.
(C) A couple on a body produce both translational and rotational motion in a body.
(D) Mechanical advantage greater than one means that small effort can be used to lift a large load.
(a) (B) and (D) (b) (A) and (B)
(c) (B) and (C) (d) (C) and (D)

P33. It is found that if a neutron suffers an elastic collinear collision with deuterium at rest, fractional loss of its energy is P_d; while for its similar collision with carbon nucleus at rest, fractional loss of energy is P_c. The values of P_d and P_c are respectively?
(a) (0, 0) (b) (0, 1)
(c) (0·89, 0·28) (d) (0·28, 0·89)

P34. In a collinear collision, a particle with an initial speed v_0 strikes a stationary particle of the same mass. If e final total kinetic energy is 50% greater than the original kinetic energy, then the magnitude of the relative velocity between the two particles, after collision, is:

(a) $\dfrac{v_0}{2}$

(b) $\dfrac{v_0}{\sqrt{2}}$

(c) $\dfrac{v_0}{4}$

(d) $\sqrt{2}v_0$

P35. A moving block having mass m, collides with another stationary block having mass $4m$. The lighter block comes to rest after a collision. When the initial velocity of the lighter block is v, then the value of coefficient of restitution (e) will be:

(a) 0.4

(b) 0.5

(c) 0.8

(d) 0.25

ANSWER KEY TO MCQ							
Q.N.	CH.	Q.N.	CH.	Q.N.	CH.	Q.N.	CH.
1	b	11	d	21	a	31	c
2	b	12	a	22	a	32	a
3	d	13	b	23	d	33	c
4	b	14	c	24	c	34	d
5	c	15	d	25	a	35	d
6	a	16	a	26	c		
7	d	17	c	27	d		
8	a,c	18	a	28	a		
9	a	19	d	29	a		
10	a	20	c	30	d		

P01: A smooth sphere A is moving on a frictionless horizontal plane with angular speed ω and centre of mass velocity v. It collides elastically and head on with an identical sphere B at rest. Neglect friction everywhere. After the collision, their angular speeds are ω_A and ω_B, respectively. Then

(a) $\omega_A < \omega_B$ (b) $\omega_A = \omega_B$

(c) $\omega_A = \omega$ (d) $\omega_B = \omega$

P02: N identical blocks are placed side by side on a horizontal frictionless surface, each two being L distance apart. At $t=0$, the first block is given a velocity V and it collides inelastically with second block and then the two blocks collide with the third and so on (all the collisions are completely inelastic) then, (ignore the size of the blocks)

(a) the centre of mass of the system moves with a velocity V.
(b) the velocity of the centre of mass is V/N.
(c) the last block moves after a time $[N/(N-1)][L/(2V)]$.
(d) the last block moves after a time $[NL]/[2V]$.

P03: An equilateral prism of mass M is kept on a frictionless floor. A particle of mass m drops on it from a height h and sticks to it. Velocity of M after the collision is: (Assume that the prism does not rebound.)

(a) zero
(b) mgh
(c) $m^2gh/(m+M)$
(d) $m\sqrt{6gh}/(2(m+M))$

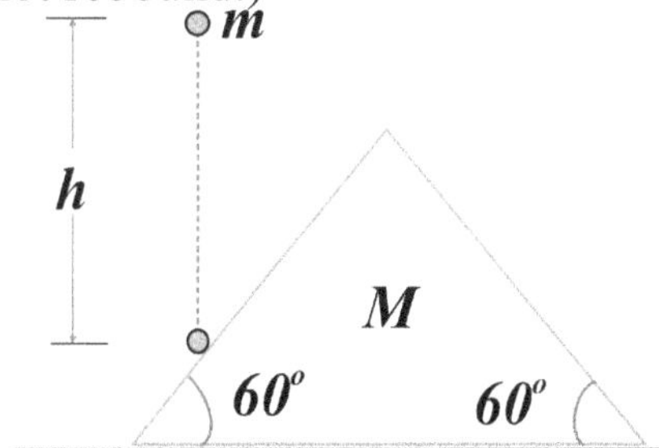

P04: In the above question, loss of mechanical energy is:

(a) zero   (b) mgh

(c) $m^2gh/(m+M)$ (d) $mMgh/(m+M)$

P05: A batsman deflects a ball of mass m by an angle of 90° without changing the initial speed u. The magnitude of impulse imparted to the ball is:

(a) 2 mu (b) mu

(c) $(\sqrt{2})\, mu$ (d) $mu/\sqrt{2}$

P06: Consider the perfectly inelastic collision of a bullet of fixed mass m and velocity v with a plank lying on a frictionless table. If the mass of the plank is increased, then:

(a) loss of K.E. increases.

(b) loss of K.E. decreases.

(c) final momentum of the whole system increases.

(d) final momentum of the whole system decreases.

P07: Molten wax of mass m drops on a block of mass M, which is oscillating on a frictionless table:

(a) if the collision takes place at extreme position, amplitude does not change.

(b) if the collision takes place at mean position, amplitude decreases.

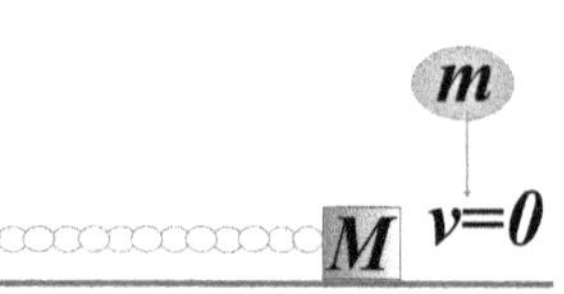

(c) if the collision takes place at extreme position, time period decreases.

(d) if the collision takes place at extreme position, time period increases.

P08: A bead of mass $2m$ can slide on a smooth straight horizontal wire. A particle of mass m is attached to the bead by a light string of length l. The particle is held in contact with the wire with the string taut and is then released. When the string makes an angle θ with the wire, the bead would have slipped a distance:

(a) $l(1-\cos\theta)$ (b) $(l/2)(1-\cos\theta)$

(c) $(l/3)(1-\cos\theta)$ (d) $(l/6)(1-\cos\theta)$

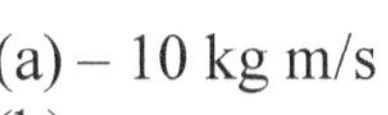 P09: A force time (F & t) plot for a linear motion is shown in the figure. The linear momentum gained between 0 sec and 6 sec is:

(a) – 10 kg m/s

(b) zero

(c) 14 kg m/s

(d) 12 kg m/s

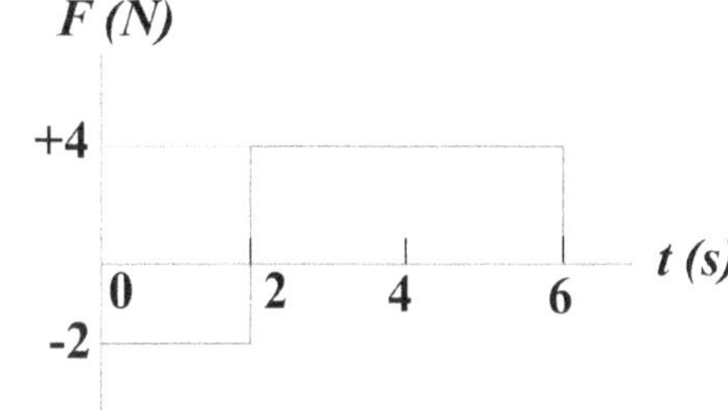

P10: In vertical circular motion of a string-bob system, during one revolution, the acceleration of the bob becomes vertical:

(a) only once   (b) twice

(c) thrice   (d) four times

P11: A body of mass m_1 collides head on elastically with a stationary body of mass m_2 and returns with one third speed over a smooth horizontal plane, then the ratio m_1/m_2 will be:

(a) 1   (b) 2

(c) 0.5   (d) 0.33

P12: A spacecraft of mass M is moving with velocity v in free space when it explodes and breaks into two. After the explosion, a mass m of the spacecraft is left stationary. What is the velocity of the other part?

(a) $Mv/[M-m]$ (b) $Mv/[M+m]$

(c) $mv/[M-m]$ (d) none.

P13: In a gravity free space, a rifle of mass M shoots a bullet of mass m at a stationary block of mass M distance D away from it. When the bullet has moved through a distance d towards the

block in the inertial frame, the centre of mass of the (bullet-block) system is at a distance of (consider recoil of rifle):
(a)*(D-d)m/(M+m)* from the block.
(b)*(md+MD)/(M+m)* from the rifle.
(c)*(2dm+DM)/(M+m)* from the rifle.
(d)*(D-d)M/(M+m)* from the bullet.

P14: A man of mass m stands on a plane plank of mass ($m/2$) lying on a smooth horizontal floor initially both are at rest. Then the man starts walking on the plank towards the east and stops after a distance l on the plank. Then:
(a)the plank will slide to the west by a distance l.
(b)the plank will continue to move towards the west over the smooth floor.
(c)the plank will slide to the west by ($2/3$) l and then will stop.
(d)the centre of mass of the (plank–man) system will remain unchanged on the floor.

P15: Potential energy of a system is given by $U(x)=(x+1)(x+2)$. Then:
(a)point $x=-3/2$ corresponds to equilibrium position of the system.
(b)points $x=-1$ and $x=-2$ corresponds to equilibrium position of the system.
(c)system is in stable equilibrium position at $x=-3/2$.
(d)system is in unstable equilibrium position at $x=-3/2$.

P16: A handball falls on the ground and rebounds elastically along the same line of motion. Then:
(a)the linear momentum of the handball is conserved.
(b)the linear momentum of the handball is not conserved, the loss in momentum being dissipated as heat in the ball and the ground.
(c)during the collision the full kinetic energy of the ball is converted into elastic potential energy and then completely converted into kinetic energy of the ball.

(d)during the collision the kinetic energy does not change.

P17: If a particle of mass m moving with a velocity v_1 is subjected to an impulse I in the direction of v_1, which produces a final velocity v_2 in the direction of v_1, then I equals: (Ignore all other forces.)

(a) $m(v_2-v_1)$ (b) $m(v_1+v_2)$

(c) $(\frac{1}{2}) m(v_1^2-v_2^2)$ (d) none.

P18: A molecule of gas 'm' flying at a velocity V elastically impinges on the wall at an angle α to the normal. Then:

(a)impulse of the force transferred to the wall is $2mV\cos \alpha$.

(b)impulse of the force transferred to the wall is $2mV\sin \alpha$.

(c)impulse of the force transferred to the wall is zero.

(d)above data are insufficient to calculate impulse of the force transferred to the wall.

P19: A particle at 9 AM is moving towards the east at 4ms^{-1}. At 12 noon, it starts moving towards the north at 4ms^{-1}. If the average acceleration of the particle during the interval 9 AM to 1 PM is a_1 and the average acceleration of the particle during the interval 10 AM to 2 PM is a_2, then:

(a) $a_1=a_2$

(b) $|a_1|>|a_2|$

(c) a_1 and a_2 are parallel to each other.

(d) a_1 is inclined to a_2.

P20: A spring of negligible mass and force constant 211 Nm^{-1} is compressed between (but not permanently attached) two blocks with masses $m_1=5\text{kg}$ and $m_2=12$ kg as shown in the figure. The blocks are initially tied together by a string and are resting on a horizontal frictionless surface. The length of the spring when compressed is 0.6 m. The string between the blocks is cut and the spring is allowed to expand. Velocity of the block of mass m_1 is 6 m/s after the blocks leave the spring. Then:

(a)velocity of m_2 is 2.5 ms^{-1} along the surface.

(b)velocity of m_2 is 3 ms^{-1} along the surface.

(c)uncompressed length of the spring once the block has moved away is 1.7 m.

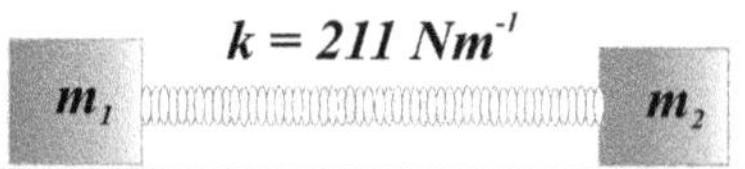

(d)uncompressed length of the spring once the blocks have moved away is 1.1 m.

P21: A ball is thrown up from a horizontal ground level at 30 ms^{-1} and at an angle 60° to the horizontal. When the ball just hits the ground, the change in its total velocity vector is very nearly equal to:

(a)60 ms^{-1} at an angle 60° below the horizontal.

(b)26 ms^{-1} downward vertically.

(c)52 ms^{-1} upward vertically.

(d)52 ms^{-1} downward vertically.

P22: A ball hits a fixed surface with a velocity u at an angle θ with the normal to the surface at the point of impact and rebounds from it at an angle β with the normal. Then:

(a) β ≤ θ

(b) β ≥ θ

(c) coefficient of restitution=e=tan θ/tan β

(d) coefficient of restitution=e=tan β/tan θ

P23: A machine gun fires 120 shots per minute. If the mass of each bullet is 10g and the muzzle velocity is 800 m/s, the average recoil force on the machine gun is:

(Assume that the machine gun is fixed.)

(a) 120 N   (b) 8 N

(c) 16 N   (d) 12 N

P24: A 200 g hollow thin-walled metal box suitably kept is hit by a 10 g bullet moving horizontally at 200 m/s. Just after emergence of the bullet, the box has a horizontal speed of 15 cm/s then the speed of the bullet just after leaving the box is:

(a) 197 m/s   (b) 340 m/s

(c) 170 m/s (d) 230 m/s

P25: A particle of mass 15 kg has an initial velocity $\vec{v}_i = 10\hat{i} - 20\hat{j}$ m/s. It collides with another body and the impact time is 0.1 s, resulting in a velocity $\vec{v}_f = 6\hat{i} + 4\hat{j} + 5\hat{k}$ m/s after the impact. The average force of impact on the particle is:

(a) $150\left(-4\hat{i} + 24\hat{j} + 5\hat{k}\right)$ N

(b) $15\left(-4\hat{i} + 24\hat{j} + 5\hat{k}\right)$ N

(c) $15\left(4\hat{i} - 24\hat{j} - 5\hat{k}\right)$ N

(d) $150\left(-4\hat{i} - 24\hat{j} - 5\hat{k}\right)$ N

P26: A light particle moving horizontally with a speed of 12 m/s strikes a very heavy block moving in the same direction at 10 m/s. The collision is one-dimensional and elastic. After the collision, the particle will:
(a) move at 2 m/s in its original direction.
(b) move at 8 m/s in its original direction.
(c) move at 8 m/s opposite to its original direction.
(d) move at 12 m/s opposite to its original direction.

P27: A ball falls vertically onto the floor, with momentum p, and then bounces repeatedly. The coefficient of restitution is e. The total momentum imparted by the ball to the floor is:

(a) $p(1+e)$

(b) $\dfrac{p}{1-e}$

(c) $p\left(1 + \dfrac{1}{e}\right)$

(d) $p\left(\dfrac{1+e}{1-e}\right)$

P28: A particle of mass m moving with velocity u makes an elastic one-dimensional collision with a stationary particle of mass m. They are in contact for a very brief time T. Their force of interaction increases from zero to F_0 linearly in time $T/2$ and decreases linearly to zero in further time $T/2$. The magnitude of F_0 is:

(a)mu/T
(b)$2mu/T$
(c)$mu/2T$
(d)none

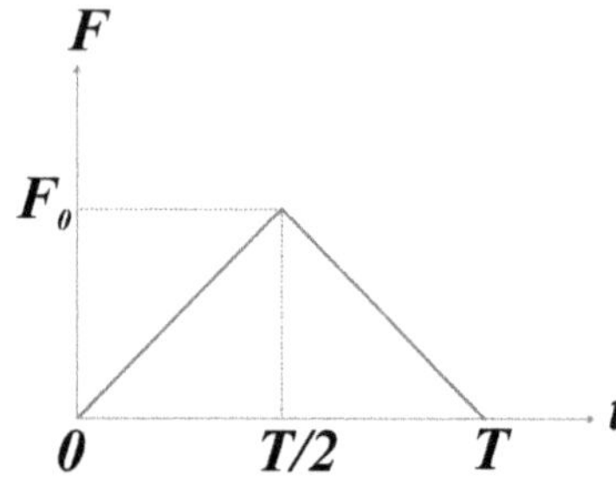

P29: A smooth sphere is moving on a horizontal surface with velocity vector $(2\hat{i}+2\hat{j})$ immediately before it hits a vertical wall. The wall is parallel to $\hat{j}$ vector and the coefficient of restitution between the sphere and the wall is e=1/2. The velocity vector of the sphere after it hits the wall is:

(a) $\hat{i} - \hat{j}$

(b) $-\hat{i} +2\hat{j}$

(c) $-\hat{i} - \hat{j}$

(d) $2\hat{i} - \hat{j}$

P30: A particle of mass m_1 makes an elastic, one-dimensional collision with a stationary particle of mass m_2. What fraction of the kinetic energy of m_1 is carried away by m_2?

(a) $\dfrac{m_1}{m_2}$

(b) $\dfrac{m_2}{m_1}$

(c) $\dfrac{2m_1 m_2}{(m_1+m_2)^2}$

(d) $\dfrac{4m_1 m_2}{(m_1+m_2)^2}$

P31: A strip of wood of length l is placed on a smooth horizontal surface. An insect starts from one end of the strip, walks with constant velocity, and reaches the other end in time t_1. It then flies off vertically. The strip moves a further distance l in time t_2.

(a)$t_2 = t_1$
(b)$t_2 < t_1$

(c)$t_2 > t_1$

(d)either (b) or (c) depending on the masses of the insect and the strip.

P32: A block of mass m is pushed towards a movable wedge of mass nm and height h, with a velocity u. All surfaces are frictionless. The minimum value of u for which the block will reach the top of the wedge is:

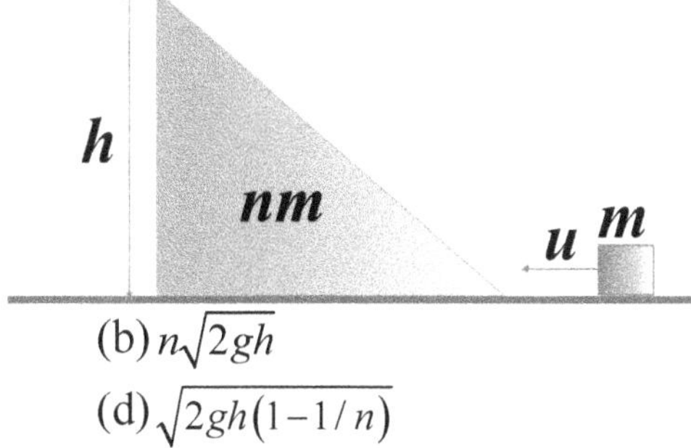

(a)$\sqrt{2gh}$

(b)$n\sqrt{2gh}$

(c)$\sqrt{2gh(1+1/n)}$

(d)$\sqrt{2gh(1-1/n)}$

P33: Two shells are fired from a cannon with speed u each, at angles of α and β respectively with the horizontal. The time interval between the shots is T. They collided in midair after time t from the first shot. Which of the following conditions must be satisfied?

(a) $\alpha > \beta$

(b) $t \cos \alpha = (t-T) \cos \beta$

(c)$(t-T) \cos \alpha = t\cos \beta$

(d)$\left(u\sin\alpha\right)t - (1/2)gt^2 = \left(u\sin\beta\right)\left(t-T\right) - (1/2)g\left(t-T\right)^2$

P34: In the figure, block B of mass m starts from rest at the top of a wedge W of mass M. All surfaces are frictionless. W can slide on the ground. B slides down onto the ground, moves along it with a speed v, has an elastic collision with the wall, and climbs back onto W. Then:

(a)B will reach the top of W again.

(b)From the beginning, till the collision with the wall, the center of mass of (B plus W) is stationary.

(c)Just after the collision, the centre of mass of (B plus W) moves with the velocity $\dfrac{2mv}{m+M}$.

(d)When B reaches its highest position on W, the speed of W is $\dfrac{2mv}{m+M}$.

P35: A strip of wood of mass M and length l is placed on a smooth horizontal surface. An insect of mass m starts at one end of the strip and walks to the other end in time t, moving with a constant speed.

(a)The speed of the insect as seen from the ground is $< \dfrac{l}{t}$.

(b)The speed of the strip as seen from the ground is $\dfrac{l}{t}\left(\dfrac{M}{M+m}\right)$.

(c)The speed of the strip as seen from the ground is $\dfrac{l}{t}\left(\dfrac{m}{M+m}\right)$.

(d)The total kinetic energy of the system is $\dfrac{1}{2}(m+M)\left(\dfrac{l}{t}\right)^2$.

P36: In a one-dimensional collision between two particles, their relative velocity is $\vec{v}_1$ before the collision and $\vec{v}_2$ after the collision.

(a)$\vec{v}_1 = \vec{v}_2$ if the collision is elastic.

(b)$\vec{v}_1 = -\vec{v}_2$ if the collision is elastic.

(c)$|\vec{v}_1| = |\vec{v}_2|$ in all cases.

(d)$\vec{v}_1 = -k\vec{v}_2$ in all cases, where $k \geq 1$.

P37: A sphere A moving with a speed u and rotating with an angular velocity ω, makes a head-on elastic collision with an identical stationary sphere B. There is no friction between the surfaces of A and B. Disregard gravity.

(a)A will stop moving but continue to rotate with an angular velocity ω.

(b)A will come to rest and stop rotating.

(c)B will move with a speed u without rotating.

(d)B will move with a speed u and rotate with an angular velocity ω.

P38: In a one-dimensional collision between two identical particles A and B, B is stationary and A has momentum p before impact. During impact, B gives impulse vector J to A.

(a)The total momentum of the 'A plus B' system is p before and after the impact, and $(p\text{-}J)$ during the impact.

(b)During the impact, A gives impulse $(-J)$ to B.

(c)The coefficient of restitution is $(2J\,/\,p)-1$.

(d)The coefficient of restitution is $(J\,/\,p)+1$.

P39: When a cannon shell explodes in midair:

(a)the momentum of the system is conserved in all cases.

(b)the momentum of the system is conserved only if the shell was moving horizontally.

(c)the kinetic energy of the system either remains constant or decreases.

(d)the kinetic energy of the system always increases.

P40: A cannon shell is fired to hit a target at a horizontal distance R. However, it breaks into two equal parts at its highest point. One part (A) returns to the cannon. The other part:

(a)will fall at a distance of R beyond the target.

(b)will fall at a distance of $3R$ beyond the target.

(c)will hit the target.

(d)have nine times the kinetic energy of A.

P41: A long block A is at rest on a smooth horizontal surface. A small block B, whose mass is half of A, is placed on A at one end and projected along A with some velocity v. The coefficient of friction between the blocks is μ. Then:

(a)The blocks will reach a final common velocity $v/3$.

(b)The work done against friction is two-third of the initial kinetic energy of B.

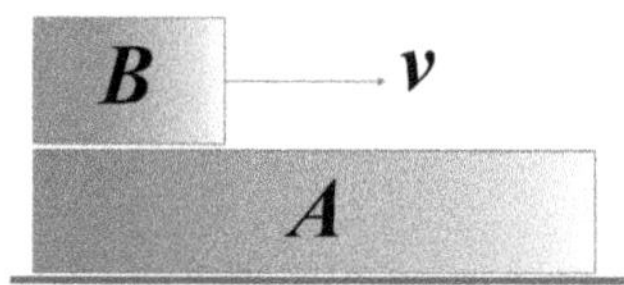

(c)Before the blocks reach a common velocity, the acceleration of A relative to B is $(2/3)\mu g$.

(d)Before the blocks reach a common velocity, the acceleration of A relative to B is $(3/2)\mu g$.

P42: A ball is dropped from a certain height on a horizontal floor. The coefficient of restitution between the ball and the floor is 1/2. In the next graph, which will be the displacement time graph of the ball?

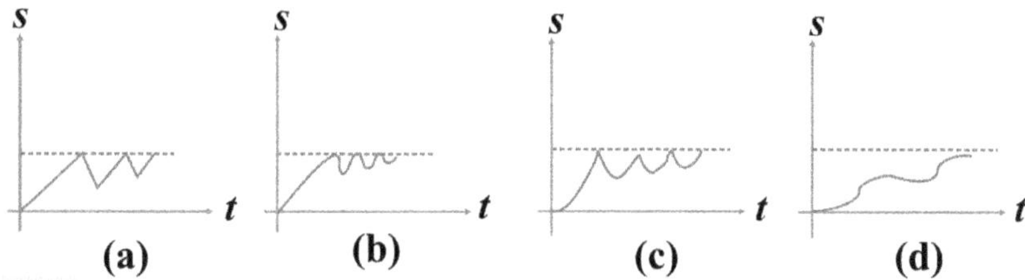

P43: The speed time graph of the ball in the above situation is:

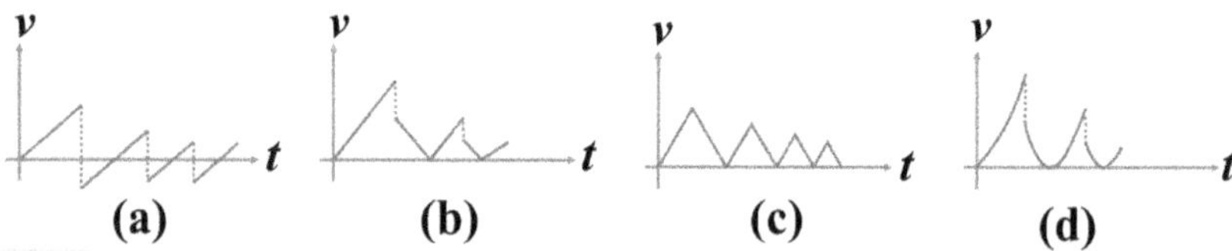

P44: A particle falls through a vertical height h and makes perfectly elastic impact with a smooth inclined plane of angle

α. The time interval between its first and second impact on the incline:

(a) is proportional to $h^{-1/2}$.   (b) is proportional to $h^{1/2}$.

(c) is proportional to $1/cos\ \alpha$. (d) does not depend on α.

P45: An isolated particle of mass m is moving in horizontal plane $(x–y)$, along the x-axis, at a certain height above the ground. It suddenly explodes into two fragments of masses $m/4$ and $3m/4$. An instant later, the smaller fragment is at $y=+15$ cm. The larger fragment at this instant is at:

(a) $y = -5$ cm   (b) $y = +20$ cm

(c) $y = +5$ cm   (d) $y = -20$ cm

P46: Two blocks of masses 10 kg and 4 kg are connected by a spring of negligible mass and placed on a frictionless horizontal surface. An impulse gives a velocity of 14 m/s to the heavier block in the direction of the lighter block. The velocity of the centre of mass is:

(a) 30 m/s   (b) 20 m/s

(c) 10 m/s   (d) 5 m/s

P47: A ball hits the floor and rebounds after an inelastic collision. If (ball+earth) system is considered as isolated, then in this case:

(a) The momentum of the ball just after the collision is the same as that just before the collision.

(b) The mechanical energy of the ball remains the same in the collision.

(c) The total momentum vector of the (ball + earth) system remains conserved.

(d) The total energy of the (ball + earth) system remains conserved.

P48: A shell is fired from a cannon with a velocity v (m/s) at an angle θ with the horizontal direction. At the highest point in its path it explodes into two pieces of equal mass. One of the pieces retraces its path to the cannon and the speed (in m/s) of the other piece immediately after the explosion is:

(a) $3v \cos \theta$

(b) $2v \cos \theta$

(c) $(3/2)v \cos \theta$

(d) $[\sqrt{(3/2)}]v \cos \theta$

P49: Two blocks A and B, each of mass m, are connected by a massless spring of natural length L and spring constant K. The blocks are initially resting on a smooth horizontal floor with the spring at its natural length, as shown in the next fig. A third identical block C, also of mass m, moves on the floor with a speed v along the line joining A and B, and collides elastically with A. Then:

(a)the kinetic energy of the (A-B) system, at maximum compression of the spring, is zero.

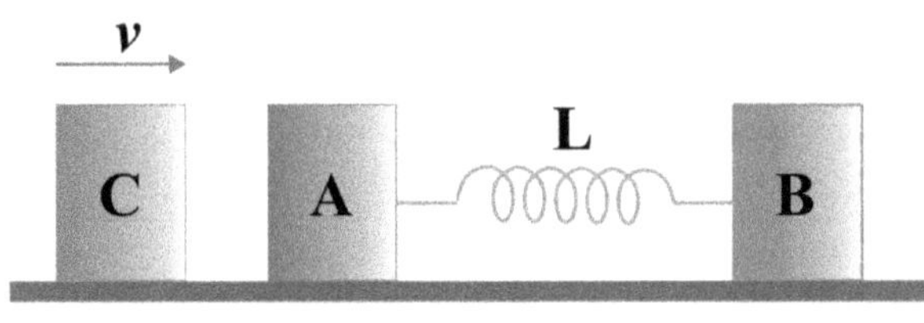

(b)the kinetic energy of the (A-B) system, at maximum compression of the spring, is $(mv^2/4)$.

(c)the maximum compression of the spring is $v\sqrt{(m/K)}$.

(d)the maximum compression of the spring is $v\sqrt{(m/2K)}$.

P50: Two balls, having linear momenta $\vec{p}_1 = p\hat{i}$ and $\vec{p}_2 = -p\hat{i}$, undergo a collision in free space. There is no external force acting on the balls. Let $\vec{p}_1'$ and $\vec{p}_2'$ be their final momenta. The following option(s) is(are) NOT ALLOWED for any non-zero value of p, a_1, a_2, b_1, b_2, c_1 and c_2.

(a) $\vec{p}_1' = a_1\hat{i} + b_1\hat{j} + c_1\hat{k}$; $\vec{p}_2' = a_2\hat{i} + b_2\hat{j}$

(b) $\vec{p}_1' = c_1\hat{k}$; $\vec{p}_2' = c_2\hat{k}$

(c) $\vec{p}_1' = a_1\hat{i} + b_1\hat{j} + c_1\hat{k}$; $\vec{p}_2' = a_2\hat{i} + b_2\hat{j} - c_1\hat{k}$

(d) $\vec{p}_1' = a_1\hat{i} + b_1\hat{j}$; $\vec{p}_2' = a_2\hat{i} + b_1\hat{j}$

Paragraph for Question No. P51 to P53: A small block of mass M moves on a frictionless surface of an inclined plane as shown in figure. The angle of the incline suddenly changes from 60^0 to 30^0 at point B. The block is initially at rest at A. Assume that collisions between the block and the incline are totally inelastic. ($g = 10$ m/s^2).

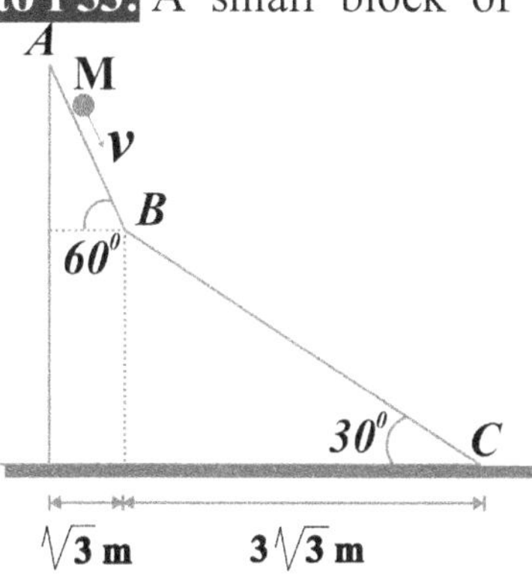

P51: The speed of the block at point B immediately after it strikes the second incline is:

(a) $\sqrt{60}$ m/s

(b) $\sqrt{45}$ m/s

(c) $\sqrt{30}$ m/s

(d) $\sqrt{15}$ m/s

P52: The speed of the block at point C, immediately before it leaves the second incline is:

(a) $\sqrt{120}$ m/s

(b) $\sqrt{105}$ m/s

(c) $\sqrt{90}$ m/s

(d) $\sqrt{75}$ m/s

P53: If the collision between the block and the incline is completely elastic, then the vertical (upward) component of the velocity of the block at point B, immediately after it strikes the second incline is:

(a) $\sqrt{30}$ m/s

(b) $\sqrt{15}$ m/s

(c) zero

(d) $-\sqrt{15}$ m/s

P54: Look at the drawing given in the below figure which has been drawn with ink of uniform line–thickness. The mass of ink used to draw each of the two inner circles, and each of the two-line segments is m. The mass of the ink used to draw the outer circle is $6m$. The coordinates of the centres of the different parts are: outer circle (0, 0), left inner circle (–a, a), right inner circle (a, a), vertical line (0, 0) and horizontal line (0, –a). The y–coordinate of the centre of mass of the ink in this drawing is:

(a) $a/10$
(b) $a/8$
(c) $a/12$
(d) $a/3$

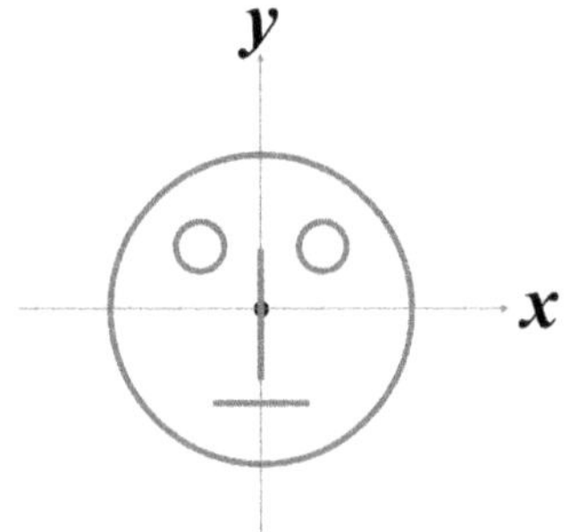

P55: Two identical particles move towards each other with velocity $2v$ and v respectively. The velocity of center of mass is:

(a) v (b) $v/3$
(c) $v/2$ (d) zero

P56: A bomb of mass 16 kg at rest explodes into two pieces of masses 4kg and 12kg. The velocity of the 12 kg mass is 4ms^{-1}. The kinetic energy of the other mass is:

(a)192 J   (b) 96 J
(c)144 J   (d) 288 J

P57: A player caught a cricket ball of mass 150 g moving at a rate of 20 m/s. If the catching process is completed in 0.1 s, the force of the blow exerted by the ball on the hand of the player is equal to:

(a) 30 N   (b) 300 N
(c) 150 N   (d) 3 N

P58: Consider a two-particle system with particles having masses m_1 and m_2. If the first particle is pushed towards the centre of mass through a distance d, by what distance should the second particle be moved, so as to keep the centre of mass at the same position?

(a) $\dfrac{m_1}{m_2}d$

(b) 1

(c) $\dfrac{m_2}{m_1}d$

(d) $\dfrac{m_1}{m_1+m_2}d$

P59: A circular disc of radius R is removed from a bigger circular disc of radius 2R such that the circumference of the discs coincide. The centre of mass of the new disc is $|\alpha|$R from the centre of the bigger disc. The value of $|\alpha|$ is:

(a) 1/6

(b) 1/4

(c) 1/3

(d) 1/2

P60: If the linear mass density λ (mass per unit length) of a rod of length 3 m is proportional to x, where x is the distance from one end of the rod, the distance of the centre of gravity of the rod from this end is:

(a) 2.5 m

(b) 1 m

(c) 1.5 m

(d) 2 m

P61: A shell of mass 200 gm is ejected from a gun of mass 4 kg by an explosion that generates 1.05 kJ of energy. The initial velocity of the shell is:

(a) 80 ms^{-1}

(b) 40 ms^{-1}

(c) 120 ms^{-1}

(d) 100 ms^{-1}

P62: An explosion blows a rock into three parts. Two parts go off at right angles to each other. These two are 1 kg first part moving with a velocity of 12 m/s & 2 kg second part moving with a velocity 8 m/s. If the third part flies off with a velocity of 4 m/s, its mass would be:

(a) 5kg

(b) 7 kg

(c) 17 kg

(d) 3 kg

Paragraph for Question No P63 to P65:

Phase space diagrams are useful tools in analyzing all kinds of dynamical problems. They are especially useful in studying the changes in motion as initial position and momentum are changed. Here we consider some simple dynamical systems in one-dimension.

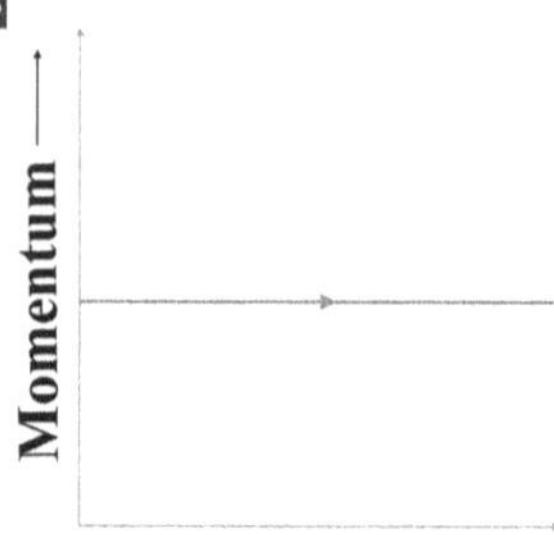

For such systems, phase space is a plane in which position is plotted along horizontal axis and momentum is plotted along vertical axis. This phase space diagram is $x(t)$ vs. $p(t)$ curve in this plane. The arrow on the curve indicates the time flow. For example, the phase space diagram for a particle moving with constant velocity is a straight line as shown in the figure. We use the sign convention in which position or momentum upwards (or to right) is positive and downwards (or to left) is negative.

P63: The phase space diagram for a ball thrown vertically up from ground is:

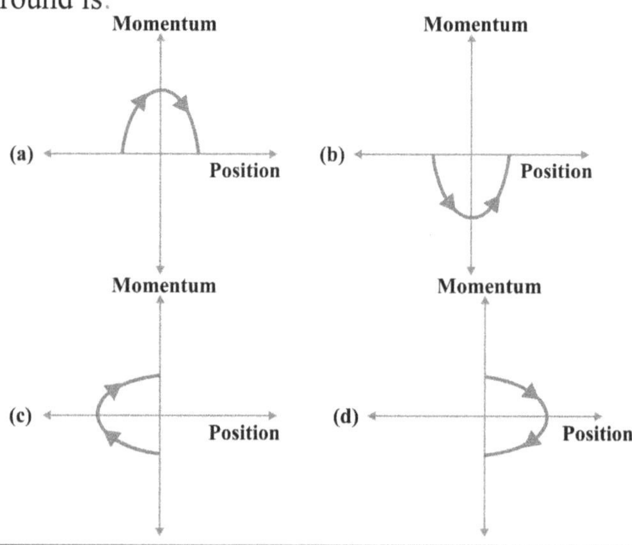

P64: The phase space diagram for simple harmonic motion is a circle centered at the origin. In the adjacent figure, the two circles represent the same oscillator but for different initial conditions, and E_1 and E_2 are the total mechanical energies respectively. Then:

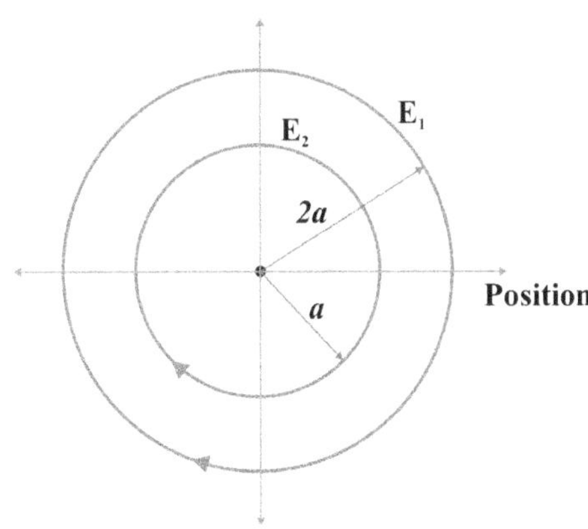

(a) $E_1 = \sqrt{2}\, E_2$

(b) $E_1 = 2\, E_2$

(c) $E_1 = 4\, E_2$

(d) $E_1 = 16\, E_2$

P65: Consider the spring-mass system, with the mass submerged in water, as shown in the adjacent figure. The phase space diagram for one cycle of this system is; for the block never comes out:

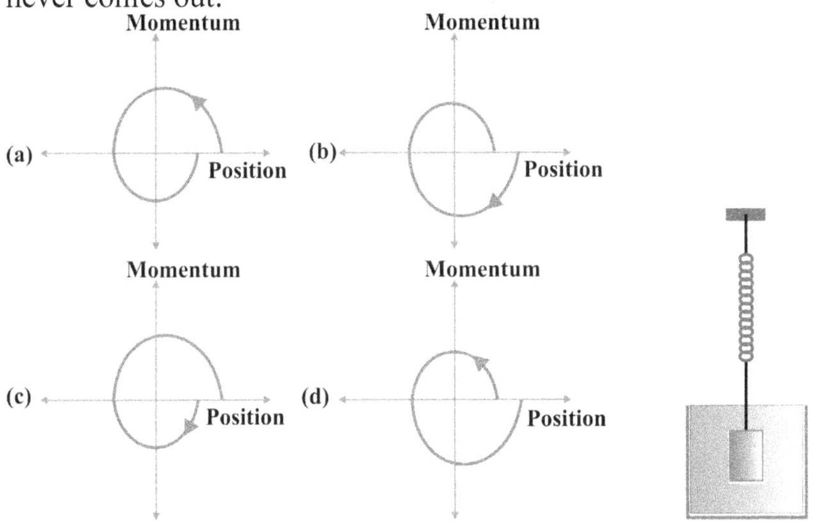

P66: A particle of mass m is projected from the ground with an initial speed u_0 at an angle α with the horizontal. At the highest point of its trajectory, it makes a completely inelastic collision with another identical particle, which was thrown vertically upward from the ground with the same initial speed u_0. The angle that the composite system makes with the horizontal immediately after the collision is:

(a) $\dfrac{\pi}{4}$

(b) $\dfrac{\pi}{4} + \alpha$

(c) $\dfrac{\pi}{2} - \alpha$

(d) $\dfrac{\pi}{2}$

P67: A tennis ball is dropped on a horizontal smooth surface. It bounced back to its original position after hitting the surface. The force on the ball during the collision is proportional to the length of compression of the ball. Which one of the following sketches describes the variation of its kinetic energy K with time t most appropriately? The figures are only illustrative and not to the scale.

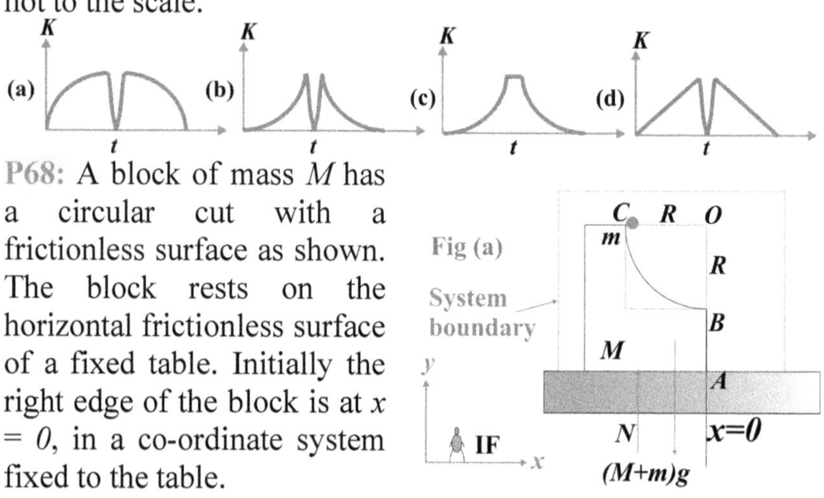

P68: A block of mass M has a circular cut with a frictionless surface as shown. The block rests on the horizontal frictionless surface of a fixed table. Initially the right edge of the block is at $x = 0$, in a co-ordinate system fixed to the table.

A point mass m is released from rest at the topmost point

of the path as shown and it slides down. When the mass loses contact with the block, its position is x and the velocity is v. At that instant, which of the following options is/are correct?

(a) The velocity of the point mass m is: $v = \sqrt{\dfrac{2gR}{1 + \dfrac{m}{M}}}$.

(b) The x component of displacement of the center of mass of the block M is: $-\dfrac{mR}{M+m}$.

(c) The position of the point mass is: $x = -\sqrt{2}\,\dfrac{mR}{M+m}$.

(d) The velocity of the block M is: $V = -\dfrac{m}{M}\sqrt{2gR}$.

ANSWER KEY TO MCQ

Q.N.	CH.	Q.N.	CH.	Q.N.	CH.	Q.N.	CH.
1	c	21	d	41	a,b,d	61	d
2	b,c	22	b,d	42	c	62	a
3	a	23	c	43	b	63	d
4	b	24	a	44	b,d	64	c
5	c	25	a	45	a	65	b
6	a	26	b	46	c	66	a
7	a,b,d	27	d	47	c,d	67	b
8	c	28	b	48	a	68	b
9	d	29	b	49	b,d		
10	b	30	d	50	a,d		
11	c	31	c	51	b		
12	a	32	c	52	b		
13	a,d	33	a,b,d	53	c		
14	c,d	34	c,d	54	a		
15	a,c	35	a,c	55	c		
16	c	36	b,c,d	56	d		
17	a	37	a,c	57	a		
18	a	38	b,c	58	a		
19	a	39	a,d	59	c		
20	a,c	40	a,d	60	d		